JOURNEY
INTO JOY

JOURNEY INTO JOY

LESSLIE NEWBIGIN

William B. Eerdmans Publishing Company
Grand Rapids, Michigan

©
1972
THE CHRISTIAN LITERATURE SOCIETY
Madras, India, and
THE INDIAN SOCIETY FOR PROMOTING
CHRISTIAN KNOWLEDGE, Delhi

First printed, 1972
First American edition, July 1973
Library of Congress Catalog Card No. 73-76339
ISBN 0-8028-1529-4

Printed in the United States of America

Preface

The following chapters originated as a series of six talks given to students and staff of the Christian Medical College, Vellore, during October 1971. The talks are given here virtually as delivered. I am very grateful to the authorities of the college for their great kindness—especially to the Reverend A. C. Oomen. I am most grateful also to Dr. Milledge who made the tape recording, and to Mrs. J. Anderson who converted it with remarkable skill and speed into clear typescript.

It is impossible to acknowledge one's debts to all those whose writings have helped to shape one's own thinking, but those who have read *The Foolishness of God* by John Austin Baker will easily recognize the influence of that fine book on the first of these lectures.

I hope that readers of these pages will be helped to go forward on that journey into joy which is the real meaning of our lives.

Contents

An Invitation

During the great part of human history it has been possible to say that, if you look at any part of human society, any nation or social group, you will find a broad agreement within that nation or group about what the good life is, about what goals are worth pursuing, about what kinds of achievement are admirable.

Of course there are rebels and dissenters in every society. And of course there is something of an age gap—in the sense that the point of view of the over-60s is different from that of the under-30s.

But what I am saying is that—during most of human history—if the over-60s in any society are talking about the good life to the under-30s, you could roughly predict what they would say.

This is not true of our society today. We are living in one of those times when there is profound disagreement among us about what goals are worth attaining, about what kind of society we ought to be trying to achieve.

In India we are living in the tension between the traditional values of the past—the values inherited from the long centuries in which the typically Indian vision of the good life was articulated—and the values associated with such words as modernization, secularization and development.

The conflict between these two is felt in every part of our lives, in families, in the relation of parents and children, of men and women, in the way in which authority is accepted or rejected, in the attitude to material things. We are profoundly influenced by ways of thinking and ways of doing things which cut right across the ways that were regarded as right and proper by our grandparents or even our parents.

Within that set of values which we indicate by such words as modernization and secularization, there are further profound conflicts and tensions. In fact we are in the midst of a worldwide crisis of goal-definition. We can indicate this by looking at the word "development." The modern use of this word is only about twenty years old. In this time we have become accustomed to dividing the world into "developed" and "undeveloped" countries—the latter being politely described as "developing" or perhaps "underdeveloped" countries. The use which has become common implies that the goal of "development" is to become like the countries which call themselves "developed"—primarily Western Europe and North America. This is the underlying assumption which controls a vast amount of the talk which fills the mass media.

But, while the so-called Development Decade has

been proceeding, we have witnessed among the most privileged young people of the "developed" countries a massive repudiation of the kind of society of which they are the beneficiaries. A few months ago I happened to be in Denver, watching the TV news. The students at the local university were staging a "Free University." One saw groups of students and teachers, sitting in the grassy meadow, talking about love and community. Around them stood a ring of National Guardsmen with guns. The scene then switched to the Governor's mansion, for a discussion with the Governor of whether he was going to issue live ammunition to these guards.

There was a scorching irony about the two scenes taken together. From one point of view one might say that it was intolerably shocking to think of using live ammunition on unarmed students who were merely talking about love. But, from another point of view, there was a kind of logic in it; these students posed a far more radical threat to society than Marxists or Black Panthers. They were not arguing about how the good things of life should be shared between the classes or races; they were totally repudiating the accepted views of what the good things of life are. These young people, and the students of the Paris revolution of 1968, and thousands of others like them, are in effect saying: what is called a modern developed society is a society in which we simply do not want to live; we have a different view of what is good. As one of the wall posters in Paris put it: "We reject the alternatives of dying of starvation or dying of boredom."

You may reply: "This is only one of the possible

models of development. There are others; there is, for example, the gigantic experiment in modernization which is the Soviet Union of today."

This is a valid reply. The Soviet model is of enormous importance. But here also there is a crisis of goal-definition. One of the most striking features of the Soviet scene today is the massive revolt of the intellectuals—especially the poets and writers—against the system. In spite of half a century of propaganda for "scientific atheism," Christianity seems to be exerting a growing attraction upon some of the most sensitive minds. The attempt to develop a more human socialism was crushed in Czechoslovakia, but the intellectual ferment which powered that attempt cannot be permanently stopped.

The point that I am making is that, in addition to the tension between the forces of tradition and the forces of modernization, there are deep divisions within the movement of modernization itself. Even if we are fully committed to a program of modernization, we do not agree about the kind of society we want to have.

We live in a time when decisions have to be made about the direction of our lives. At other times and in other societies these questions did not have to be raised; there was agreement about what is the goal and what was needed was the determination to reach it. Today we are in the midst of a crisis of goal-definition. Which way ought we to be going?

I was born and bred in a city where the chief industry was shipbuilding. Among the professions listed in the telephone directory was that of "compass-adjustor.'' When a ship is built and the compass is fitted, it is necessary to employ a skilled professional to adjust the compass in order to compensate for the magnetic attraction of the steel-work of the ship. To do that, the ship—after it is launched and fitted out—is taken to some quiet bay, away from anything that might affect the compass, where this adjustment can be done. After that, the ship can go to the ends of the earth, and the master will know that the compass gives him true directions.

These chapters are meant to provide an opportunity for that sort of compass-adjustment. It is an opportunity to take time, away from other distractions, to become clear about direction, about goals.

You may rightly ask what qualifications I have for doing this job. Am I as a compass-adjustor? You will certainly find as you read that there are plenty of questions to which I do not know the answers. As I grow older I am less inclined to be dogmatic about many things. But there are a few things about which I am sure. I am sure about Jesus Christ. That is why I dare to take part in a mission like this.

Forty-two years ago there was a student at Cambridge who was not a Christian believer, but who was very much concerned about the way the world was going and his responsibility for it. This student decided to spend a good part of his first long vacation working with the miners of the Rhondda Valley in South Wales, who had been rotting in unemployment and misery for a decade. The experiment was not a success. But one night, overwhelmed by the sense of defeat and of the power of evil in the world, there was given to him a vision of the cross of Jesus Christ as the one and only reality great enough to span the distance between heaven and hell, and to hold in one embrace all the variety of humankind, the one reality that could make sense of the human situation.

I was that student. During the years that have followed I have been trying to work out the meaning of that cross for human life. I do not know all the answers, but I am quite sure that this is where the answers are to be found. I invite you to share with me in exploring the meaning of the cross of Jesus Christ for the journey that we have to make.

The Mystery
of Life and Faith in God

If you have read the story of Scott's expedition to the South Pole, you will remember that there was one occasion on that terrible journey when, owing to some kind of mist that descended upon them when they were crossing an absolutely flat and featureless plain of snow, they found themselves in a situation where they could see nothing. They could not see even a line of horizon. There was nothing but a blank white wherever they looked, up or down, left or right. And as they went on, trying to continue their journey, they found that they were going round in circles. They found themselves coming back again on their track in the snow. They had to find some way of leading the dogs forward. So they hit upon the device of throwing snowballs ahead of them in the direction in which they had to go, and following the snowballs.

A good deal of our life is spent like that. We cannot really see anything in the distance. There are no land-marks. But we have what we call "projects." Project is made up of two Latin words which mean "something thrown forward." We throw forward an idea. I will get into college. I will pass an examination. I will acquire this degree. I will get this job. Or perhaps it is a much bigger project. We will set a man on the moon within the next ten years. We will find a cure for cancer. It may be a small project or a big one. The point is that a project gives us a sense of direction. As long as we are working for that project, we know where we are going. We are not going around in circles.

But when we have got there—when we achieve the project—what next? How do we know whether what we have achieved is worth having? Has it brought us any nearer to a goal which is worth getting to? Scott's men knew in which direction to throw their snowballs, because they had a compass which enabled them to determine true South. Do we have a compass? Do we know what is the direction that will ultimately take us anywhere when we have finished all our projects? Is there a direction which is really forward? Is progress a meaningful word—taking the human situation as a whole? Of course there is progress in this or that field of knowledge, or technics, or research. But is there progress in respect of our whole human situation? Is this world a better, a kinder, a more humane, a more just place than it was fifty years ago or five hundred years ago? Or are we just going around in circles, coming back again on our track like Scott's men in the Antarctic?

As you know, a great many of the world's philosophers have said that we are doing exactly that, that human life is a series of cycles, that we go around, but come back again to the same place. Indeed that is a very obvious explanation of human life, because we see it in nature. We see flowers, animals, plants, human beings, societies, and institutions, which are conceived, born, grow, become mature, grow old and perish. If we look at nature, this is what seems to happen, and therefore it is natural that we should also interpret human life that way. Existence is a great wheel, the wheel of nature. It goes around and gives us the illusion of movement, but eventually brings us back to the place where we started. And therefore, according to this kind of thinking, the wise man will seek to escape out of this ceaseless wheel of change. But we must ask—to escape into what? Is the escape worth having? What is worth having?

In asking all these questions, am I asking a lot of unnecessary and meaningless questions for which there are no answers? Some people would say that I am, but I cannot help asking these questions, at least sometimes. And I am not ashamed of asking these questions, because I know that we grow up only by asking questions. A child in its earliest infancy does not ask questions, but takes things for granted. But the day comes when it begins to say "Why? Why? Why?" It exhausts its parents by an innumerable series of questions about everything and everybody. And yet we know that it is by asking questions that the child grows.

This is true not only of the child. The great scientist Lister said that the beginning of science is the art of making oneself strange to the familiar, of looking at what is familiar with new eyes, like Newton looking at the apple falling from the tree and asking "Why does this apple fall?" To make oneself strange to the familiar, to ask questions about what most people take as obvious and don't ask questions about—this is the beginning of knowledge.

I say, I'm not ashamed to ask these questions. Nor am I ashamed to say about many of them, "I don't know the answer." The man who knows all the answers is already dead, for practical purposes. He will learn nothing. We must ask questions. But they must be serious questions. They must be questions which we ask because we want the answer. There are some people who go about asking questions but are not interested in the answers. We must ask questions with the same kind of interest as a traveler who has lost his way.

Well, where do we begin to answer questions like this? Do we have a compass? I believe we do. I believe that it is in Jesus Christ and the faith concerning him that we can find the sense of direction which our lives have to take if we are to get anywhere. But obviously, also, you are not going to accept this because I say so. Nor should you accept it. You should only accept it if you see for yourself that it is true.

Of course, there is a stage when you accept things because somebody tells you so. In our childhood we accept the fundamental beliefs of our parents without asking questions. We do not even ask what these beliefs are. They are just part of ourselves. Just as at the beginning the physical life of the child is part of the physical life of the mother, so also for a much longer period our mental life is part of the life of our parents. It is not just that we say, "My father says so and therefore it must be." We only begin to say that when we have already begun to think a little for ourselves. There is an earlier stage when we think, we value, we believe, we judge, simply because that is the way we have been made and brought up.

But, just as the umbilical cord must be cut, and just as the child must be weaned, so also, with equal necessity, if we are to become adults, we have to ask our own questions and make our own decisions. It will not be enough for us even to say "The Bible tells me so," because we have to face the question, "Why and how is the Bible an authority for me? Why must I accept what the Bible says?"

Well, once again, how do we begin answering this kind of question? We can only begin with our own experience; not our individual private experience, but the experience of the human race in which we share, especially of its greatest and most sensitive representatives. The answers to great questions are not obvious. They are not shouted at us, or written up in the sky. We cannot find them by buying a handbook at the bookstore. We have to take risks if we are to understand the really important things. We have to look, to listen, to ponder, to reflect, to experiment, and ultimately to take risks—to risk our very selves. The answers to great questions have to be struggled for.

But what, then, are the most significant things in our experience? What are the things of which we are bound to say, they are good, precious, lovely in themselves; we do not have to argue about their goodness, because we know they are good? What are the things that make life worth living?

Of course different people will answer that question in different ways, and the same person in different ways at different times in his life. But there are some things that we surely could all say are good. There is the experience of beauty in nature, the beauty of a flower, of a sunset, of a woman's face. There is beauty in art, of a line of music, of poetry, of a sculpture. There is the simple experience of good health, of the contrast between hard work and leisure, the contrast between the all-out effort to win a race or climb a mountain and the rest that follows. There is the feeling of cold water swilling over your body and clean clothes after you have been hot and dirty. There is the experience of friendship, of the loyalty of friends and colleagues, of the love of man and woman. There is trust, one of the most precious of all human experiences, the trust of friends. There is the experience of pure goodness in another person—courage, kindness, patience, joy—glimpsed, thank God, in the life of a friend or through a book or a film.

These things are good in themselves. We do not need to argue whether they are good or not to justify them. If life contains these things, then to that extent it is good. It is not futile, but worth living.

But there is another side to the picture. These good things do not last. Some are fleeting, given to us only for a moment. Some are more enduring. All come to an end. The flower fades, the sunset's glow vanishes. The loved one must die and all the most precious things of our experience are finally engulfed in the darkness of death.

But it is not only that these things are transient. The world is full of things which contradict and violate all our sense of beauty and goodness. It is full of ugliness and discord. The songs of the poets are drowned by the electronically amplified rantings of politicians and demagogues. The lovely human body is wrecked and slowly destroyed by a malignant cancer. The trust of a friend is betrayed for thirty pieces of silver. The brilliant young student is killed in a meaningless accident. The honest man is punished and degraded, and the swindlers and the scoundrels are rewarded with honors and offices.

How can we believe that such a world has any meaning? Why not curse God—if there is one—and die?

That was the advice that Job's wife gave him in the middle of his agony. The story of Job is one of the marvelous treasures of the Bible. I advise you to read it in the New English Bible. I think you will not put the book down till you have finished it. Job is a man of perfect integrity—upright, kind, and magnanimous. He is the victim of a series of appalling catastrophes. Within a few days he is bereaved of all his children, utterly ruined, and smitten with a loathsome disease. From the depths of his misery he cries out to God in protest: "Why have you done this? It is not just and you know it is not just."

These cries of Job shock his pious friends who have come to comfort him, and they try to smother his protest with all the usual religious arguments: God cannot be unjust, so these catastrophes must be punishment for your sins. You think you are a righteous man, but it is obvious that you are really a very great sinner. Indeed, the fact that you looked like such a righteous man and now have had this appalling series of catastrophes shows that you were really a hypocrite. Only now your real character comes out, now that you are blaspheming against God. Keep quiet and humbly accept what God sends.

Here is the language of one of Job's comforters:

> Come to terms with God and you will prosper;
> that is the way to mend your fortune.
> Take instruction from his mouth
> and store his words in your heart.
> If you come back to the Almighty in true
>   sincerity,
> if you banish wrongdoing from your home,
> if you treat your precious metal as dust
> and the gold of Ophir as stones from the
>   river-bed,
> then the Almighty himself will be your
>   precious metal;
> he will be your silver in double measure.
> Then, with sure trust in the Almighty,
> you will raise your face to God;
> you will pray to him, and he will hear you,
> and you will have cause to fulfil your vows.
> In all your designs you will succeed,
> and light will shine on your path;
> but God brings down the pride of the
>   haughty
> and keeps safe the man of modest looks.

He will deliver the innocent,
and you will be delivered, because your hands
*   are clean.*

Job 22:21-30.

All very pious language. But Job brushes it aside. He says: I want to meet God face to face so that I can put my case before him, get justice from him because I am in the right. This is Job's answer:

My thoughts today are resentful,
for God's hand is heavy on me in my trouble.
If only I knew how to find him,
how to enter his court,
I would state my case before him
and set out my arguments in full;
then I should learn what answer he would give,
and find out what he had to say.
Would he exert his great power to browbeat me?
No; God himself would never bring a charge
*   against me.*
There the upright are vindicated before him,
and I shall win from my judge an absolute
*   discharge.*

Job 23:1-7.

Job does not use any of the pious language of his friends. He wants to get justice from God. And you know the end of the story, so completely different from what you would expect. When God comes on the scene it is to rebuke and condemn the pious friends and to vindicate Job. Not that God answers Job's questions. He doesn't. They remain unanswered. The point is that God's presence and blessing is given to the man who persists in saying "Why?," the man who cries out for justice, the man who protests against the evil of the world, and not to the pious people who would smother all these questions with a lot of premature religious answers.

The point is that there is a mass of bitter human experience to contradict all the things that seem to make life worth living. There is a mass of experience which makes us question whether there is any meaning at all or whether it is just

> *A tale told by an idiot,*
> *full of sound and fury,*
> *signifying nothing.*

If you reach that point in the argument, what is the next move? If you find that things are in a mess, one obvious move is to say, "Who is responsible for this mess? Call him and tell him to clear it up." But this is a rather sophisticated move. Small children, for example, and men in the early stage of development which we call animism don't make this distinction between things and persons. A small child does not distinguish between a person who is responsible and things which are not. A child will scold a doll, or get very cross with something on the floor that trips him up. So also primitive man, the "animist" as we call him, does not distinguish between what is living and not, and he sees trees and mountains as living things to which he can address his prayers. As you well know, most people who own automobiles become animists when their cars won't start, and begin to curse the unfortunate vehicle. That is the primitive stage of man's existence.

The next stage is reached—and it had been reached by the time of the most ancient recorded writings that we know of—when the personality is seen to reside not in the thing itself, but in a realm above the natural world, in what we call a supernatural world. This is the world of divine beings, of gods and goddesses who influence or control the events of the natural world, who preside over different parts of it. There is no one being responsible for everything. Not at all. In Hindu religion there is a multitude of devas, who control the different sectors of life. There are gods of fire and water and wind, there are gods of earth and sky and sea, there are gods of sex and money and learning. These divine beings may be good or bad, benign or mischievous. Indeed, they played in the ancient world the same role that film stars play in our world, that is to say, they provide another world on to which we can project all the desires which we would like to fulfil and cannot. But these gods and goddesses are not ultimately responsible. Finally they are also under the control of something else—whether it is called Fate or Karma or what you will. But this view of life also, while in some ways it gives a kind of explanation of our human experience in all its diversities and multiplicities, cannot be finally satisfying. There cannot be a satisfying meaning for life as a whole for us, made as we are, unless in some sense someone is finally responsible.

And in the ancient world only one people, among

all the people of the world, dared to assert and cling to the faith that one is finally responsible. I mean the Jews. Persian religion sought to give meaning by seeing the world as a struggle between good and evil powers. Greek thought tried to separate God from the world, believing that the absolutely good could not be mixed up with the evil world. Indian spirituality sought meaning by escaping altogether from the world of the senses. It was only Judaism which dared to assert that this whole visible, natural world, as well as whatever invisible worlds there may be, is created and ruled by one God who is good and wise and holy. And when disaster following disaster fell upon the Jewish people, they still clung to that belief, interpreting these disasters as being not a defeat for God, but rather as God's punishment for them for their sins. That is something absolutely unique in all human history.

But is this view tenable? Apparently not. In this world in which good and evil are so completely mixed up, which at one moment seems to make sense and in another moment is nonsense, what is the meaning of saying that one is responsible? If God alone is responsible, either God is also immoral and irrational, or else some way must be found by which his character as good and rational can be vindicated in spite of all the evil and irrationality in the world.

If that is to be done, then there are two possible moves. The first would be the move made by Job's comforters. This seems to be an unjust world, but actually that is an illusion. Really you are being punished for your sins, or perhaps your parents' sins, or perhaps the karma of your previous incarnation is catching up with you. So don't protest. Don't complain. To protest and complain is just unbelief and blasphemy. Humbly accept and submit yourself to what comes; don't rebel against it. Submit yourself to God and all will be well. If you are suffering, it is because of your sins; repent of your sins and all will be well. That was the advice of Job's friends, which he rejected. He would rather go on vehemently protesting and questioning even in his agony and humiliation than accept that solution. And the message of the Book of Job is that God is on the side of Job and not on the side of his so-called comforters.

The second possible move is a different one. We can put it in its simplest form in this way: we can say, yes, the world does not make sense now, but it will make sense in the end. There is a meaning, there is a plan, there is one who is responsible, but you are part of the plan. Your response, your belief, your commitment to the plan, your loyal participation in carrying it out—these are all essential elements in the rationality of things, and without these they will not be rational.

In other words, it is possible to sit back as a spectator of the whole scheme of things and say, "It does not make sense. Either there is no one in charge, or if there is anyone in charge he is neither moral nor rational. You can count me out." But it is also possible to take another position. It is possible to believe that there *is* one who is in charge, and that I can hear and accept his invitation to join him in changing things. It is possible to believe in the vision of a world which *will* make sense, in which all the misery and pain that we know now will be seen to have been worth it for the sake of what was to be done. We can sum this up in words which you will recognize as the words of Karl Marx, who in some ways understood the Bible better than most Christians did. He said our job is not just to understand the world, but to change it. And he further said that there is no possibility of understanding the world except by being actually involved in changing it.

Please note the point we have reached in our argument. We have not proved anything. We have only indicated the possibilities. Looking at the mess which the world seems to be, we have said first of all, "Is anyone in charge here? If he is, he must be either stupid or bad." And we have said that there are two possible ways of meeting that. One is the way of Job's comforters. The other is the way which looks to the future and says: "This is a mess because the job is not yet finished. If you will come and lend a hand and accept the master plan, you will begin to understand why it is this kind of mess and what it is that is being made. As you share in making it now, and as you enjoy the triumph when it is finished, you will see that it does make sense."

Now again, I say we have not proved anything. We have indicated a line along which we shall explore in the chapters of this book.

Just to round this off let me say this. Of course there are other possibilities which I have not touched on. One could think that the world is just a vast and complex mechanism of which I am simply a part. But that lands one in insuperable logical difficulties. In the first place a machine is by definition a device contrived by human beings to carry out certain purposes. The idea of a self-generating machine which exists for no purpose is a logical absurdity. Secondly, if I am part of a machine and my thoughts and actions are mechanically produced by the interaction of material particles, then all questions become absurd because there can be no wrong or right answer but only the calculable result of the mechanical process.

Or one could think that everything was an organic process, analogous, for example, to the growth of a tree. But there again, the same argument applies. If I am simply part of a process, then questions are absurd. I am what I am and I think what I think because I am part of the process and cannot be otherwise.

Or there is again the third possibility. It is possible to accept the view that all that happens is the working out of karma—the karma that I have earned in previous births. This means that a kind of explanation is given for the appalling injustices of human life. There is therefore a kind of rationality, but it is rationality purchased at an appalling cost. For, if this is true, then the one thing that no one can ever do is to bear the karma of another. No one can help his friend to bear the load of pain and sorrow. If this theory is true, each man's karma must ineluctably find him out and no one else can interefere. And that means that one of the most precious of all the things that do make life worth living, namely the love that is willing to die for a friend, is excluded. And that is too high a price to pay for rationality.

What we have tried to do is this, only to indicate the possibility of finding meaning in life in terms of a purpose, a plan, which is not yet fulfilled, but which calls for our cooperation, of which our cooperation is an essential part.

In closing, let me say a word about this line which we are going to explore in the coming essays. In the first place I think you will see that this line, this way of proceeding, provides a basis for rationality, not in terms of contemplation but in terms of action, not in terms of theory but in terms of practice. It is as we are committed to and involved in this plan, this purpose, that we can begin to understand its meaning. And therefore there is a basis for hope.

This is a simple point, but a very fundamental one, and I want to enlarge upon it a little. We are very familiar in our generation with protest as a fact of social life. Hardly a week passes without some kind of protest, some kind of demonstration. A procession is taken out, something is burned; there is some kind of protest against things as they are. This is the most vivid way in which we can express our belief that this world as we know it is not the last word, that there is something which transcends this world, something more, something different. But what *is* that thing which is different? The trouble about those protests, as we know, is that most of them peter out. The ordinary world, the world of power, the world where power politics rules, appears to be the only thing that is real. The world of the protesters appears to be a kind of ideal world, a world which does not exist except as a vision in their own heads. So that it seems to be a battle between the real and the unreal, and the real always wins. The vision is real enough. But if it is only in my head, if it is not yet realized in outward fact, what is its reality?

But if we know in our own experience that something can be real which is not yet realized—a plan, a purpose, a hope—could that not give us the clue which we are seeking to the rationality of things as a whole? If the ultimate cause of all things were such a vision, such a plan, which is only slowly being realized, this would explain why we are haunted by a reality which is different from, greater than, the world that we know, which, in the language of theologians, is "transcendent." This idea of transcendence is always very difficult: how can there be anything which is other than what I actually experience? How can anything exist which is other than what is actually accessible to observation? But if we follow this clue, we can see that there is a kind of transcendence: there can be something real which is not yet realized. It is real, because it is God's plan. But it is not yet realized, because God is infinitely patient.

The second thing about this line of reasoning is this. I said a few pages above that the Jews were the only people who dared to hold on to their faith that there is one responsible for all that is and for all that happens, and that the appalling disasters that fell upon the Jews one after another were interpreted as punishment for their sins. But that led to an impasse. How are we to understand what seem to be the monstrous injustices of life? I said there are two ways in which one could try to understand. One is the way of Job's friends: whatever the evidence is, the fact must be that if you are suffering you must be a sinner. The other alternative is the patient, dogged, enduring faith that somehow, some time, God would vindicate himself.

The Book of Job is one of the great expressions of that faith in the Bible. Another most wonderful expression of it is in the Psalms, where you will find that faith struggling against the wickedness and irrationality of the world. But above all there are those marvelous passages in the second part of the Book of Isaiah, where the poet sings of a servant of the Lord whose suffering will not be meaningless suffering, but will be a willing bearing not of his own sins, but of the sins of others.

> *Yet on himself he bore our sufferings,*
> *our torments he endured,*
> *while we counted him smitten by God,*
> *struck down by disease and misery;*
> *but he was pierced for our transgressions,*
> *tortured for our iniquities;*
> *the chastisement he bore is health for us*
> *and by his scourging we are healed.*
> *We had all strayed like sheep,*
> *each of us had gone his own way;*
> *but the LORD laid upon him*
> *the guilt of us all.*

Isaiah 53:4-6.

It was this vision of the servant of the Lord bearing the sin of others which was accepted and embodied in his own person, by one greater than Job, by Jesus of Nazareth. And that acceptance took him to the cross.

The whole New Testament is a working out of the meaning of that cross, and it ends with that very strange book, the Revelation of St. John, which is an imaginative picture of world history centered in the figure of a lamb, a sacrificial lamb that has been slain. It is in terms of that vision that the New Testament finds meaning and rationality, in a world that is so full of unreason and injustice. The ultimate secret is nothing other than the patient and long-suffering love which bears the sin of the world and bears history itself to its glorious conclusion. The lamb slain from the foundation of the world is on the throne.

That is the vision of the meaning of human existence, which is embodied in the book that we call the New Testament and which we shall explore in the remaining chapters.

2

Jesus Christ

We were seeking to find some sense of direction in life. How and where, amid the irrationality and injustice with which the world is filled, do we find a clue to rationality?

I indicated one line of inquiry, namely the idea of a purpose which is real but not yet realized. It is that line which we will inquire into as we go along. At this point I want to make three remarks about it. The first is this, that it helps us to explain the tension that we all feel in our experience between things as they are and things as they ought to be. This is an ever-present element in our experiences. Sometimes it explodes in protest when we say these things ought not to be. But then we are thrown back on the question, What is there? What really exists apart from what we see, with all its injustices and irrationality? If, when we speak of what ought to be, we are not speaking of just a dream in my mind, but of the reality which in truth shapes all things, of what "the one in charge" really intends, then this would explain the feel of reality which this has.

The sense of reality about it comes because it is what the one who is responsible intends. Then we can understand this tension, neither side of which we can get rid of, between what is and what ought to be.

Second, it means that if we follow this clue, the sense of rationality becomes possible only, insofar as we are involved in action, in realizing the plan. Indeed, we can only understand in so far as we are committed.

Third, it means that hope becomes a central part of human life and not just delusion, as so much of the world's religion has taught.

I said that this line of thought had its starting point in the unique faith of the Jewish people. Alone among all the peoples of the ancient world, the Jews, in face of all the irrationalities, the injustices and disasters that are our human lot, stubbornly insisted that there is one responsible, one in charge, who is both wise and good. We are now to explore the meaning, for this line of thought, of the life and teaching, death and resurrection and subsequent place in history of one man who belonged to the Jewish people and who was the heir of their faith, the man whose Jewish name was Joshua, and who is known to the world (because his greatest disciples wrote in Greek) by the Greek form of that name—Jesus.

We are especially concerned with him because at the center of his story there is an event which challenges, more sharply than any other event in history, the view that this is a rational and just world. Jesus was executed by crucifixion and thereby branded by his contemporaries as an accursed criminal and an enemy of God. How is it that this event, the most irrational and unjust event in all recorded human history, has become the central point of the faith that human history is being guided towards the fulfilment of a just and rational purpose?

To begin with we can ask the question, How much can we know about Jesus? There are a few people who have tried to prove that Jesus never existed. But that can be safely put aside as a crazy theory for which no responsible scholar will stand for a moment.

The earliest scrap of evidence from a non-Christian source about Jesus is the sentence of the Roman historian Tacitus of the first century, who talks about the "followers of one 'Chrestus,' who was executed as a criminal under Pontius Pilate, but whose followers alleged that he was alive." That is very early evidence of the central fact about what is believed about Jesus. There is also very early reference in a Jewish writer on one Jesus, "who was a magician who led many people astray." Apart from these scraps of evidence, all our evidence about Jesus comes from his followers, who believed that he was indeed alive. How reliable is their evidence?

There are vast numbers of ancient manuscripts in which it is embodied. As you know, until the fifteenth century when printing was invented, there was no means of reproducing records except by hand. There are thousands of manuscripts preserved. Many of them are from the eighth and ninth centuries. There are a few which are much earlier. There is one manuscript of the New Testament dating from the fourth century, and there are a number of manuscripts of the second century containing part of the New Testament. As a result of the vast labors of scholars over two centuries, it can be stated with confidence that, in spite of some variations between the manuscripts, there is an astounding degree of accuracy in transmission. If you compare the King James Version of the Bible, which is based mainly on ninth- and tenth-century manuscripts, with the modern translations, which are based on the much earlier manuscripts, you will see how small the differences are.

When were these records written? The earliest of our four Gospels, the Gospel of St. Mark, was written about forty years after the events it describes, and is generally believed to be based on the memories of Peter. Twenty years earlier than that we have the letters of Paul, evidence of the belief of the Christians of the first generation. And before there were any of these written texts, there was what we call the "oral tradition." Stories about what Jesus did and said were remembered and repeated by his disciples. They were not written down to begin with, because the first disciples expected the very early return of the Lord and the end of the world. These stories naturally developed a certain standard form, just as the jokes that we tell. We never bother to write them down because we remember them. Once we have heard a good story we don't forget it; but there is a certain form in which we remember it. So with these ancient stories of Jesus, what he did and what he said were also preserved in standard form. But naturally also, during the twenty years or so in which these stories were circulating, in the great centers where there were very strong Christian communities—Jerusalem, Antioch, Ephesus, and Rome—these stories took slightly different shapes. And later on, when in each of these centers the stories were collected together and written down, these collections contained variations from one another. And when these different collections were brought together in different combinations to form what we call our four Gospels, naturally some of these differences remained. There were other gospels also, based on ancient traditions, but the church felt they were not so reliable as evidence of what had happened, and gradually discarded them.

As a result of the vast critical labor of the last two centuries, a great deal has been done to disentangle the different sources which have gone to make up our Gospels. Some of the critics have been more intelligent than others. Some have been clever; some have been wise. Some have been radical; some have been conservative. But the total result of their efforts is that we now have a much clearer and more vivid picture of Jesus than we have ever had before.

This kind of criticism is necessary. If we believe that we are dealing with what really happened, that we are dealing with real history, we must be prepared to have it examined and criticized as openly as possible. If we resist that claim, it would look as if we do not believe in the real historicity of these events.

The main result of all these great critical labors, in spite of a number of absurd theories and wild speculations, has been that the facts about Jesus stand out much more clearly and vividly than ever before. If you compare the theological writing of today with that of two centuries ago, you will see that, as compared with the clear, vivid picture of Jesus which we have in our writing today, the Jesus who appears in the theological books of two centuries ago is much more like a kind of theological cipher—somebody who performs a theological function, but is not a living person.

Can we try to bring before our eyes, before our minds, a picture of this person?

Perhaps one way to do it is to take one of the Gospels, like the shortest one, St. Mark, and sit down and read it right through at one sitting. You can easily do it in one hour. Read it right through from beginning to end, then put it down and ask yourself what kind of man was this. You will receive a tremendously vivid impression. No one can read that Gospel right through, even if he has read it many times before, without getting a tremendously vivid impression of what kind of person Jesus was.

One of the earliest efforts to put this into a few sentences is in what Peter said to Cornelius when he was first asked to speak about Jesus. You will remember these words which come in the tenth chapter of Acts: "I need not tell you what happened lately all over the land of the Jews, starting from Galilee after the baptism proclaimed by John. You know about Jesus of Nazareth, how God anointed him with the Holy Spirit and with power. He went about doing good and healing all who were oppressed by the devil, for God was with him. And we can bear witness to all that he did in the Jewish country-side and in Jerusalem. He was put to death by hanging on a gibbet. But God raised him to life on the third day, and allowed him to appear, not to the whole people, but to witnesses whom God had chosen in advance" (10:37-41).

I want to take this as a starting point and just suggest to you in a few brief headlines, some of the essential facts about Jesus, which stand out clearly in the record and which remain unchallengeable after all these centuries of critical examinations.

There is first of all the simple phrase that is used by Peter. *He went about doing good.* The coming of Jesus was like the breaking in of a divine power into the human life. You remember that when John sent messengers to ask, "Are you the one whom we expect, or do we still have to wait for another?" Jesus said, "Go and tell John what you see. The blind see, the deaf hear, the lame walk, the lepers are cleansed, and blessed is he that does not stumble because of it." In other words these things are signs that the reign of God has broken into the life of men. The freeing of the oppressed, and good news, therefore hope, to the poor—that is the first thing that the coming of Jesus meant.

The second thing, and this is one of the very striking features of the story, is that Jesus made friends of those whom society cast out. It was constantly said in criticism that he ate and drank with publicans and sinners. Publicans were those to whom the Romans farmed out the business of tax-collecting. They were, in other words, the stooges of the colonial power. And they made a very good profit out of it, because under the Roman system the tax-collecting was let out to contractors, and the contractor would squeeze as much as he could out of the people and take his commission and pass on as little as possible to the government. So these publicans were in two senses hateful. They were stooges of the foreign power, and they were profiteers, exploiting the people. And regarding the other group, called "sinners," the records make it clear that it includes prostitutes and people whom the ordinary decent people of the country would not associate with. Here was a man, who talked like a guru but kept company with the most disreputable people that you could think of. And when he was challenged about it, he told those three stories about the lost sheep, the lost coin, and the two sons, by which he explained why it was that he had to keep that kind of company. On the other hand, this Jesus was so sharp in his criticism of the religious leaders of his time, that we can hardly bear to read his words: "brood of snakes," "whitewashed tomb-stones," "blind guides of the blind," and other equally cutting denunciations of those who were regarded as the upright and the good.

The third thing that stands out in the records about Jesus is that he forgave sins, and that this caused great shock. You remember the story of the four men who let a man down through the roof because they could not get near Jesus any other way. The story says that Jesus, seeing their faith, looked at the man on the bed and said, "Son, your sins are forgiven." It is not that this was a kind of general theological declaration; it was an authoritative word that caused the people sitting around to be shocked, and to accuse Jesus of blasphemy. Of course I can forgive sins which are done against me. But this man had not done any sins against Jesus; it was the sins against God that Jesus was forgiving. Jesus, with the authority of God, forgave sins and authorized his disciples to do the same.

The fourth thing that is clear from the record is that Jesus, when necessary, would break the laws of his people. He broke the minor laws about food and washing. He broke the major law of the Sabbath, the most fundamental of all the Jewish laws. But when it conflicted with the needs of men, Jesus without hesitation broke it, and said, "The Sabbath was made for man, and not man for the Sabbath." This is the most radically secularizing remark that it would be possible to make. Even more shocking was that he attacked the very basic idea on which the Sabbath rested, that is to say, the idea that God had completed the work of creation in six days and then had rested. When he was challenged "Why are you doing this on the Sabbath day?" he said "My Father has never stopped working, and I am working."

Fifth, he spoke with an authority which appeared to be blasphemous. He quoted the divine commandments from the Old Testament and then coolly added, "But what I say to you is this"—and then said something radically different. He spoke of those who would be ashamed of his words being put to shame on the day of judgment. And he said "Whoever loses his life for my sake and the gospel shall find it." He made, quietly, claims which appeared to his contemporaries to be blasphemous.

Sixth, he both claimed and concealed the claim that he was the Messiah. The Messiah, which means the "anointed one," was the one whom the Jews expected to come at the end to make sense out of the mess, to be the agent of God in bringing all things to their true conclusion. Jesus pointed to his works of healing, and said, "Blessed is the man who does not find me a stumbling block"—in other words, who can recognize in these things the presence of the Messiah. He does not announce himself as the Messiah, but happy is the man who recognizes him. Then at Caesarea Philippi when Peter recognized him, Jesus ordered him to tell no one. At the end, by riding into Jerusalem on a donkey, a kind of acted parable, he challenged those who had eyes to see to recognize who he was.

And finally, Jesus had a unique sense of Sonship. The word "Abba," the Aramaic word for "My Father," appears again and again in the Greek text of the New Testament. Obviously, the Greek readers did not know what it meant, because on every occasion the Greek writer translates it "Abba, Father." That word had become so precious in the ears of Jesus' disciples, that the very syllables that they heard so constantly from his lips had to be reproduced even when they were writing about him in another tongue. This is a rock-hard piece of evidence about something which was central in the life of Jesus—this utterly intimate relationship with his father. Jesus could address God in a way that no Jew had ever dared to address him. No trace of such a usage is to be found in any Jewish prayerbook or liturgy before the days of Jesus. And he always talked that way; that was the way he spoke to God: "My Father." It was the most intimate kind of expression which a child could use in speaking to its father. At the very end, in the agony on the cross, it was his last word, "Father, into your hands I commit my spirit."

This, then, is the man who was crucified under Pontius Pilate. Why was he crucified? And what has this to do with our search for meaning in life?

The first thing to be said about this is that we know about Jesus because he was raised from the dead.

All the material that we have in the New Testament, which means, practically speaking, everything that we know about Jesus, is written by those who believed that Jesus had died and had been raised from the dead, and it would not have been written otherwise.

There were thousands of Jews who were crucified in the hills of Judea during the Roman occupation. In fact, there was a complaint that the country was becoming deforested because the demand for wood for crucifixion was so great. Only one or two of their names have come down to us. Of the vast majority of them we know absolutely nothing. We know about Jesus because thousands of people who knew that he had been executed, that he had died, and that he had been buried and that he had been in the tomb for two days, were sure that he was alive, and that he had told them to tell the world that he was alive.

It is clear from the record that even his closest friends did not understand what he was doing. Even up to the moment of the cross, they were quarrelling with one another about chief places in his kingdom. Even the closest of the disciples, Peter, was so unable to understand what was happening that he denied him at the last.

Some writers have said that what really happened at Easter was that the disciples were so impressed by Jesus, so sure that he couldn't die, that the belief that he was still alive was generated in their minds as a kind of fantasy which came to be accepted as reality.

There are two things to be said about this. First, it contradicts the evidence. It is clear from the evidence that before the cross, the disciples did not understand what was going to happen, and that after the resurrection they were not willing to accept it. It is a strange fact that theological writers constantly repeat the statement that the risen Jesus did not appear to any of his enemies, but only to his friends. This is of course not true. The very first evidence that we have of the resurrection of Jesus is in the letters of Paul. And we know that Paul was indeed an enemy of Jesus, and that it was as an enemy persecuting the church that he was confronted and stopped in his tracks by a vision of the risen Lord, and that that was the whole basis of his becoming a Christian. Second, it needs to be said that if this theory is true, the whole Christian faith rests on an illusion. To the question: Was Jesus right in what he did? Was he right to trust God the way he did? we would have to answer: No, he was mistaken.

The whole story in the New Testament is written, as I have said, from the point of view of the resurrection, and the Christian faith is inexplicable otherwise.

Another point to be made is that the story of the resurrection is not told in the New Testament as the story of a victory which wipes out the defeat of the cross. On the contrary, there is great emphasis laid on the fact that the risen Lord is the crucified one. It is said that when he showed himself to his disciples, he showed them his hands and his side. In other words he identified himself deliberately to them as the one who had been crucified. And according to the records that we have, in his teaching of them, he emphasized the fact that it was necessary for the Messiah to suffer in this way. Above all in Paul, whose life as a Christian began with a meeting with the risen Lord, it is nevertheless the cross which is the center of his message. The cross, in other words, is not put before us as defeat overruled by God; on the contrary, the cross is put before us as a victory which was acknowledged and ratified by God.

The cross in itself, in other words, is good news. How can that be? What did the cross mean for Jesus? And what does it mean for us?

We saw that Jesus regarded himself, in some sense, as being the Messiah. This is one of the things we can be sure about from the records. Remember the background of this word Messiah. This background is the faith of the Jewish people, to which I have referred over and over again, that there is one responsible, who is wise and good. This faith had to struggle against all the frightful power of wickedness, all the evidence that this world is not just and reasonable, but unjust and mad. And we saw that one possible way of meeting this problem was to hold on to the faith that somehow, some time, God would vindicate his own righteousness; that his wise and good rule which is not manifest now would become manifest; that all the mess would be cleaned up and all men would see what the plan had been and that it was a good plan, worth all the blood and tears that had gone into it. At the center of this hope, there was the vision of the Messiah, the anointed one, the one who would come as God's representative to establish his just and wise rule.

The Messiah was pictured in many different ways in the Old Testament, as we know.

There is the picture of the military hero who will destroy all the enemies of Israel, as we find it in the Second Psalm:

> *Of me he says, 'I have enthroned my king*
> *on Zion my holy mountain.'*
> *I will repeat the LORD's decree:*
> *'You are my son,' he said;*
> *'this day I become your father.*
> *Ask of me what you will:*
> *I will give you nations as your inheritance,*
> *the ends of the earth as your possession.*
> *You shall break them with a rod of iron,*
> *you shall shatter them like a clay pot.'*
> *Be mindful then, you kings;*
> *learn your lesson, rulers of the earth:*
> *worship the LORD with reverence;*
> *tremble, and kiss the king,*
> *lest the LORD be angry and you are struck down*
> *in mid course;*
> *for his anger flares up in a moment.*
> *Happy are all who find refuge in him.*
>
> Psalm 2:6-12.

Here is another picture, the wise ruler, the son of David, the one like David:

Then a shoot shall grow from the stock of Jesse,
and a branch shall spring from his roots.
The spirit of the LORD shall rest upon him,
  a spirit of wisdom and understanding,
  a spirit of counsel and power,
  a spirit of knowledge and the fear of the
    LORD.
He shall not judge by what he sees
nor decide by what he hears;
  he shall judge the poor with justice
  and defend the humble in the land with
    equity;
  his mouth shall be a rod to strike down the
    ruthless,
  and with a word he shall slay the wicked.

Isaiah 11:1-4.

Then there is the more mysterious figure of the later Isaiah, who rules not with the rod of iron, but by suffering:

Here is my servant, whom I uphold,
my chosen one in whom I delight,
I have bestowed my spirit upon him,
and he will make justice shine on the nations.
He will not call out or lift his voice high,
or make himself heard in the open street.
He will not break a bruised reed,
or snuff out a smouldering wick;
he will make justice shine on every race,
never faltering, never breaking down;
he will plant justice on earth,
while coasts and islands wait for his teaching.

Thus speaks the LORD who is God,
　he who created the skies and stretched them
　　out,
who gave breath to its people,
　the breath of life to all who walk upon it:
I, the LORD, have called you with righteous
　　purpose
　and taken you by the hand;
　I have formed you, and appointed you
　to be a light to all peoples,
　a beacon for the nations,
　to open eyes that are blind,
　to bring captives out of prison,
　　out of the dungeons where they lie in
　　darkness.
I am the LORD; the LORD is my name;
　I will not give my glory to another god,
　　nor my praise to any idol.
　See how the first prophecies have come
　　to pass,
　and now I declare new things;
before they break from the bud I announce them
　　to you.

Sing a new song to the LORD,
　sing his praise throughout the earth,
　you that sail the sea, and all sea-creatures,
and you that inhabit the coasts and islands.
Let the wilderness and its towns rejoice,
　and the villages of the tribe of Kedar.
Let those who live in Sela shout for joy
　and cry out from the hill-tops.

You coasts and islands, all uplift his
     praises;
   let all ascribe glory to the LORD.
The LORD will go forth as a warrior,
he will rouse the frenzy of battle like a hero;
he will shout, he will raise the battle-cry
     and triumph over his foes.
   Long have I lain still,
I kept silence and held myself in check;
now I will cry like a woman in labour,
     whimpering, panting and gasping.
I will lay waste mountains and hills
     and shrivel all their green herbs;
I will turn rivers into desert wastes
     and dry up all the pools.
Then will I lead blind men on their way
and guide them by paths they do not know;
I will turn darkness into light before them
     and straighten their twisting roads.
All this I will do and leave nothing undone.
   Those who trust in an image,
Those who take idols for their gods,
     turn tail in bitter shame.

   Hear now, you that are deaf;
you blind men, look and see:
yet who is blind but my servant,
who so deaf as the messenger whom I send?
Who so blind as the one who holds my commission,
     so deaf as the servant of the LORD?
   You have seen much but remembered little,
your ears are wide open but nothing is heard.

*It pleased the LORD, for the furtherance of his
         justice,
to make his law a law of surpassing majesty;
yet here is a people plundered and taken as
         prey,
all of them ensnared, trapped in holes,
    lost to sight in dungeons,
carried off as spoil without hope of rescue,
as plunder with no one to say, 'Give it back.
Hear this, all of you who will,
listen henceforward and give me a hearing:
who gave away Jacob for plunder,
    who gave Israel away for spoil?
Was it not the LORD? They sinned against him,
they would not follow his ways
    and refused obedience to his law;
so in his anger he poured out upon Jacob
his wrath and the fury of battle.
It wrapped him in flames, yet still he did not
         learn the lesson,
scorched him, yet he did not lay it to heart.*

                                        Isaiah 42.

Jesus was the heir to these messianic hopes. He lived
among people who cherished these hopes as the one
thing that made life worth living. And according to the
record it would seem that he became sure of his vocation to be the Messiah at his baptism. But at that
moment it was not the texts from the Psalm or Isaiah
11 that sounded in his ear, but it was the words of
Isaiah 42: *This is my beloved child, my servant, in
whom I am well pleased.*

If Jesus knew from that moment that he was called to the greatest of all possible tasks, to be God's Messiah, then he had first of all to wrestle alone with the awesome question: How can that task be fulfilled? Away in the solitude of the desert he fought that question through. One after another the different ideas of what God's Messiah would be were considered and discarded—the clever politician who gets a following by satisfying the crowd; the wonder-working holy man who dazzles with supernatural powers; the Zealot who takes a shortcut to justice by using a gun and a bomb. All these were rejected, and Jesus came forth from the desert as the unarmed Messiah—armed only with one thing, an absolute and unshakable trust in the one whom he had known since his first conscious moments as Abba, my Father, my own Father.

How, then, does he fulfil the role of Messiah? Quite simply, by being the son of his Father, by doing the works of his Father. His deeds and words are the deeds and words of God. There is not a program or a campaign for changing the world. Only the deeds of God are done—which are the deeds of love; and the words of God are spoken—which are his promises of grace. The sick are healed, the blind are given sight, the deaf ears are opened and cripples are given power to walk. Men burdened by guilt, men burdened by the load of sin, are released by a word of forgiveness spoken with God's own authority. Those who are hopelessly lost are sought out and loved back into hope and joy. The works of God are being done before men's eyes. And what can this mean except that the Kingdom of God is at hand, on the threshold? The whole people of God must be roused to hear and believe this unbelievably good news.

As I said a moment ago, Jesus does not openly proclaim himself as Messiah. A few only catch the secret—like Peter, who with breathless daring blurts it out for the first time: "You are the Messiah." And Jesus strictly warns him to keep it to himself. If Jesus is announced publicly as the Messiah, the people, who have their own very clear ideas about what the Messiah will be like, will try to force him into their pattern, as indeed they did after his feeding of the five thousand. Only near the end, by riding into Jerusalem on a donkey, in fulfilment of the ancient prophecy of Zechariah, did he give a hint for those with eyes to see. And in the end, in the final scene before the Jewish court, in answer to the direct question, he confessed that he was the Messiah.

But during his ministry it was his secret. He wanted men to see for themselves that the powers of God's kingdom were already at work in their midst. To those who were looking everywhere for signs of the Kingdom he said: "Don't look for signs, the Kingdom of God is here and now among you—in your midst."

But they could not see it. The words of Isaiah were proved true:

> *You shall look and look and not see.*
> *You shall listen and listen and not hear.*

Gradually admiration and enthusiasm turned to opposition and hatred, as people found that their most prized possessions and convictions were coming under attack. Jesus was like a blazing light which first of all attracted people, and then, because it exposed all the hidden filth, became unbearable, so that they all combined with one murderous intent to blot the light out. You know the story, how finally all the forces that were usually opposed to one another—the modernizing Pharisees, the conservative Sadducees, the time-serving Herodians, the Roman political authorities, the common people—all finally combined to destroy him.

But what did it mean for him? Again I remind you that the Gospels were written in the light of the resurrection. The Gospel writers insist that Jesus knew that he was going to die and rise again. But they also repeat again and again that the disciples did not understand. It is quite clear from the record that they were totally unprepared for the cross when it came, and that they were not able to believe the resurrection. Surely Jesus must have tried to prepare them, above all by his words at the Last Supper. But whatever Jesus said to them it was not enough to make them understand. We must think that it was not quite as simple and clear as it seems afterwards in the light of what happened on Easter morning.

That Jesus knew he was going to be rejected is clear. But that it was an agonizing disappointment is also clear. There is the cry when he looks over the city of Jerusalem and says: "O, Jerusalem, Jerusalem, the city that murders the prophets and stones those sent to her; how often would I have gathered your children together under my wings, but you would not." And there is the agony in Gethsemane: "Father, if it be possible, let this cup pass from me." And there is the cry of dereliction on the cross: "My God, my God, why hast Thou forsaken me?" These were surely real words of agony and dereliction. Jesus was not play-acting. The writer of the letter to the Hebrews, more than any other New Testament writer, has understood this part of the gospel story most vividly. Jesus, he says, tasted death for every man. Jesus was the pioneer and perfecter of our faith.

In other words, Jesus, who was the loving and beloved child of God, and who was called to be God's Messiah, the one through whom God's rule was to be established in the world, lived, suffered, and died right to the very end in a simple trust in his Father. He committed everything into his Father's hands, even when his whole life work was in ruin, when his people had rejected his call, when his own disciples had left him, denied and betrayed him and, most terrible of all, when he was to undergo that particularly horrible and degrading death which carried with it the curse of God: *Cursed is he who hangs on a tree.*

We must believe that Jesus tried to assure his disciples that because everything was in the Father's hands, everything would be well. We may guess that many years later when the disciples wrote down what they remembered, they made it seem that his predictions were more clear and precise than they were. But from the record it is clear that what happened on Calvary was this: the one and only man who has ever lived in total fellowship, trust, and obedience towards God, met the concentrated power of human sin, and in committing everything totally and simply into his Father's hands, bore it all to the end, praying for his murderers, and finally committing himself into his Father's hands, whom he had loved from the beginning.

It was this Jesus whom God raised from the dead. The resurrection was not just the resurrection of somebody. It was the resurrection of Jesus. And, to put it at its simplest, this must mean at least these three things:

First of all, the God whom Jesus trusted as his Father is real, more real than death.

Second, this God who is the real God is the God whose nature was reflected and revealed in what Jesus was, did, and said. In other words, to use the language that I used earlier, the one who is in charge is like that, and he is really in charge.

Third, the thing Jesus began to do must go on. He is the Messiah, and God's rule is what is manifested in his life and deeds and words, the rule of the one who is really in charge. This, then, is the clue to the future. In the language of the Easter hymn: "The powers of hell have done their worst." The ultimate depths of evil and irrationality have been plumbed by the death of Jesus. There is absolutely nothing more that the powers of evil can do; there is nothing more to be feared. We can with sure confidence join ourselves to him and share in his continuing work of making the Father's will known and done throughout the whole creation. In that work, life is given a meaning which neither evil nor death can destroy.

3

New Life in the Spirit

We talked in the preceding chapter about the death and resurrection of Jesus as the central point of the Christian interpretation of human experience. At this point, we believe, the deepest questions of human life are exposed and settled—the questions of good and evil, and of life and death.

The death of Jesus is the naked, unarmed encounter of pure goodness with all the forces of evil. Jesus refused to make the slightest compromise with evil in any form in order to avoid that head-on collision. He followed to the end the path of complete loving obedience to the loving purpose of his father, even to the point of praying for the forgiveness of his murderers.

The death of Jesus is also the point at which the injustice and irrationality of the world are at their blackest. Here the defeat of goodness and victory of evil are seen at their extreme development. In the death of Jesus the obliteration death brings to all human achievement is seen in its most devastating form.

The death of Jesus would be that and no more if it were not for the fact of the resurrection. In the light of Easter morning we begin to understand that Jesus on his cross, Jesus praying for his enemies, Jesus battling with pain and shame until the moment when he cries out in triumph "It is finished," Jesus in his dying is the very power and wisdom of God himself; that the father to whom Jesus committed himself in loving obedience is indeed the one in whose hands all things are, the one responsible, the one whose purpose is the only meaning that life has.

To put it in another way: we mentioned the instinct to protest in all of us. There is something in us all which refuses to accept things as they are, which demands change, which says, "Even if the evil institution has existed for a thousand years, it must go. It is an insult to man." There is something in all of us which rebels, which protests against things as they are in the name of things as they ought to be.

We are familiar with particular protests, protests against war, against social injustice, against male domination, against racism.

The life and death of Jesus is the one total protest against all things as they are which we have seen in human history. And in the resurrection we see that protest endorsed, validated. The one in charge is on the side of the protester and not of the establishment. The protest is not a futile gesture. It is not like the protest of the suicide, an act of despair. It is an act of hope and faith—faith in God and hope for his Kingdom. The resurrection is the sign that solid reality is on the side of Jesus and not on the side of the worldly-wise and powerful men who destroyed him.

But how does one come to believe in the resurrection? Millions don't believe. It is impossible to explain. All kinds of unanswerable questions arise, if we begin to discuss the resurrection. As a historian you may be convinced that nothing except the resurrection can explain the event that followed the death of Jesus. As a physicist you may have to say that this is simply impossible. It is very important that we face this frankly.

The fact is that when we come to talk about the resurrection, we are not simply talking about one fact which we could try to fit into the sum total of our experience. We are, so to speak, on the boundary of our experience. We are dealing with something which, if it is true, is the starting point of a wholly new way of understanding and organizing our experience.

The resurrection cannot be fitted into any view of the world except one of which it is itself a total starting point, because the resurrection is the validation of a protest against everything that there is. It is the same point which I made earlier. The cross is the ultimate protest against things as they are, in the name of what ought to be.

Jesus staked everything on his faith that the world as it is is not God's last word, that a new and different world is possible and that a new and different world is what the Father intends. The resurrection is God's validation of that faith. Therefore the resurrection is to be understood and explained not by showing how it can be fitted into the experience that we already have of the world as it is. It is, rather, to be understood and explained by showing how it opens up the possibility of new experience, of new powers and victories, and ultimately of a new world.

To put it in other words, the lines of explanation, the lines of rational coherence by which we can connect the resurrection with the rest of our experience and make with it a part of a coherent whole do not stretch backward into the past but forward into the future. The resurrection is a boundary line, a point at which two worlds touch. One is the world which ends in the cross. The cross is the ultimate summary of unredeemed human experience, the final victory of human blindness and prejudice, the final victory of death. The cross is the point to which ultimately all the roads that we know lead. The resurrection is the beginning of a new world, a world which opens out into infinite new possibilities and ultimately to the vision of a renewed and redeemed creation, new heavens and a new earth, a new Jerusalem, a new humanity.

Some of you may have read Lewis Carroll's charming story "Alice Through the Looking Glass." Alice was a little girl who lived in a big house, and in the biggest room of the house there was a great big mirror. Alice used to look through this glass to see the room on the other side of it, which was very much like the room which she was in, but the other way round. It had doors leading out of it and she longed to go through these doors to explore the passages beyond. And it had a window, and she longed to go through that window, and go and explore the hills which she could see. It was the fascination of another world which began just at the point where this world stopped.

What we have in the cross and the resurrection is something like that. It is the point at which one world stops and another world begins.

But how do you get through the mirror? Alice just walked through that looking glass in her dream. In real life you can't just walk through. The witness of the New Testament writers is that you go through that looking glass only at the cost of your life. In a very real sense you come to the end of your life and start again; you have to die and be born again.

But how? The most complete and vivid description of what it means to go through that looking glass is given in the life of a man called Saul of Tarsus, who is known to history as Paul the Apostle. Paul was a man of two worlds. He had behind him all the strict training of an orthodox Jew in his mother tongue, at the feet of one of the most famous rabbis of his day in the city of Jerusalem. He was at the same time a man of cosmopolitan education. He spoke and wrote in Greek and he was a Roman citizen.

Saul was a passionately devoted Jew. He knew enough, cosmopolitan as he was, about the pagan world to know the contrast between the strength and cleanness of the Jewish way of life and the filth and folly of that Hellenic world. He cared with all his heart and soul that his nation should fulfil its God-given role in world history by a life of righteousness which would prepare the way for God's reign. In his own life he set himself the strictest standards of personal righteousness.

To such a man the Christian preaching was an abomination and a blasphemy. Jesus was a false pretender to the title of Messiah, misleading the masses, undermining the most sacred institutions of religion, subverting the standards for which the prophets and martyrs had shed their blood. Jesus had met his proper end: he had been crucified. And it stands written in Holy Scripture: "Cursed is he who hangs on a tree." Jesus was accursed. But now to have this accursed blasphemer placarded throughout the world, and especially in the Jewish synagogues, as the true Messiah, was a blasphemy beyond endurance. Such pestilent propaganda must be stopped once for all. And to that task Saul devoted all his great powers.

We know what happened. In mid-career he is stopped in his tracks by a blinding light, and a voice that questions him, "Saul, Saul, why do you persecute me?" Not able to look up, Saul whispers the question. "Who are you, Who are you?" And the answer is, "I am Jesus whom you are persecuting."

The accursed one is the Lord of glory—the living and regnant Lord. Saul's world is turned upside down. Saul himself is not a servant of God but an enemy of God. The crucified Jesus, the accursed Jesus, is the living God, and those who crucified him are the enemies of God.

Such a shattering reversal of all that he had lived and struggled for needed time to think out. Saul went away into the desert, as Jesus had done, to think it out, and find out what it implied. And when he came back, he was a man for whom the cross had become the luminous center of all his experience. In a dozen different ways in his many letters he tries to tell what the cross means. One of the simplest and clearest comes from that autobiographical passage in the letter to the Galatians in which he is explaining his own experience and defending himself against the charge that he is a bogus apostle. After he has spoken of his experience on the Damascus road and in the days that followed, he says this:

> For through the law I died to law—to live for God. I have been crucified with Christ: the life I now live is not my life, but the life which Christ lives in me; and my present bodily life is lived by faith in the Son of God, who loved me and gave himself up for me.

> Galatians 2:20.

You see that he is saying three things about what it means to go through that mirror. First he says, "I have been crucified with Christ." That is what it means to come to the end of the road marked by the cross. The old Saul, the Saul that men knew as a brilliant, assured, confident fighter for the Kingdom of God, died that day on the Damascus road. That was the end of the road for this man who was sure that he was on the side of God. He knew now that his zeal, his assurance, his piety, his self-righteousness were not of God, but were the very opposite. They were enmity against God. It was these things in fact that had crucified the Son of God. The death of Jesus is the death sentence for Saul.

He died, but the death is mine. I have no longer any right to live. The sentence of death is pronounced on me. This is the end of the road.

Second, another road begins. He died, but he lives. And he died for me, and therefore the life that he lives is for me. The death that was my due he accepted for himself. He died in order that I might not die, and therefore, the life that I now live is his gift. It is not my life but his. Saul is dead. There is no future for Saul; that road leads nowhere. It ended at the cross. The life that I now live from that day onwards is simply his gift to me. He who died and lives, lives in me. His life is given to me as a gift renewed every day.

Third, I know that this is a new life, for its basis, its principles, its goal, are quite different from the old. Its basis, its starting point, is that the Son of God loved me and gave himself for me. Its starting point is that amazing gift, and therefore its goal is simply to give thanks for that amazing gift. Its goal is not any more that I should be a good man. That has been given up. There is no future for me as a good man. I am no longer the center of the picture. The goal is Jesus—that he should be glorified. And its principle is faith—faith which looks away from myself to him, faith which simply relies completely on what he has done and will do.

In the verse we read we have Paul's autobiographical description of what the new life means, of what is meant to go through that looking glass. It is put in the first person singular because Paul is being personally attacked as a false apostle, and he has to defend himself. But he makes it clear in many places, as the New Testament does, that in fact this new life is a profoundly corporate affair. It is the life of a community and it can only be lived in a community. The whole point of it is that the "I," the ego, has been removed from the center of the stage. Life is now an offering in gratitude to Jesus—and that means, therefore, that it is a shared life, shared with all those who acknowledge the same debt to Jesus. Even Saul, when he reached Damascus, had to be received and blessed by another disciple, Ananias, and then by baptism taken into this fellowship of those who were already of the company of Jesus. That proud ego was not broken down just to start a new life on its own, lived in a private relationship with Jesus. Not at all. It was to be an open life, a life shared with brethren, shared with all those who owed and acknowledged the same debt.

This common life did not start with Paul. It was there already, and he was welcomed into it by the disciples of Damascus. It was something which began immediately after the resurrection of Jesus, when the first disciples had been through the same kind of experience that Paul had gone through on the Damascus road—the experience of being utterly broken, utterly defeated, utterly humiliated, the experience of having come to the end of the road, and then the experience of finding that there was a wholly new road opened in the fellowship of the risen Jesus.

We have two accounts in the New Testament of how this fellowship began. One of them is in the twentieth chapter of the Gospel of John:

> Late that Sunday evening, when the disciples
> were together behind locked doors, for fear of
> the Jews, Jesus came and stood among them.
> 'Peace be with you!' he said, and then showed
> them his hands and his side. So when the disci-
> ples saw the Lord, they were filled with joy.
> Jesus repeated, 'Peace be with you!', and said,
> 'As the Father sent me, so I send you.' Then he
> breathed on them, saying, 'Receive the Holy
> Spirit! If you forgive any man's sins, they stand
> forgiven; if you pronounce them unforgiven, un-
> forgiven they remain.'
>
> John 20:19-23.

When Jesus breathes upon his disciples and says
"Receive the Holy Spirit," he is saying to them, "My
life from now on is your life." The breath is the life, as
the Old Testament repeatedly says. When breathing
stops, life ends. In the language of the Old Testament
the one word *ruach,* translated both as breath and as
spirit, refers in the first instance to the breath of God,
which is the life of God, which is the Spirit of God.
God had given his Spirit in a special way to prophets
and kings and heroes of the past. He had given his
Spirit in all its fulness to his beloved Son. Now,
through the Son, the same Spirit, the same breath of
God, the same life of God is given to the disciples to be
the stuff, the power, of their corporate life. They will
not be just a set of individuals each living his own life
and pursuing his own goals. Their life will be the life of
Jesus, shared in common. And the marks of that life

will be that they are bearers of peace and of forgiveness.

The other account of how this common life began is found in the second chapter of Acts, in the chapter that records the events of the day of Pentecost. Here the picture is somewhat different. It is more dramatic. There is wind and fire and noise, and the disciples immediately rush out of the room into the streets talking in strange tongues so that the passersby think that they are drunk.

Before we look at the differences between these two accounts, it is good that we look first of all at the things which they have in common. Both of them are descriptions of the way in which this common life began. And they have two things in common.

The first is that the Spirit is given to a community. In the Old Testament, when we read of the gift of the Spirit, it is normally given to an individual. (The only exception that I can remember is the story of the seventy elders in the Book of Numbers.) In the New Testament it is always to a community, to a group. It is true that we have two cases, Barnabas and Paul, where an individual is described as being filled with the Spirit. But, nevertheless, at the great turning points where the coming of the Spirit is described it is always to a community.

The second point which these two accounts have in common is that the Spirit is given for mission. "As the Father sent me, so send I you. Receive the Holy Spirit," said Jesus. And so also at Pentecost the gift of the Spirit issued in the power of communicating a message to men of every race and tribe. Some of the puzzling features of the Book of Acts become clearer if you understand this, that the gift of the Spirit is always for mission, is always the equipping of God's people for their witness to the world, exactly as the gift of the Spirit to Jesus at his baptism was his anointing for his mission as the Messiah.

However, we cannot close our eyes to differences between these two accounts. And these differences are reflected in the later parts of the New Testament and in the history of the church. In the New Testament and in the later church, there have been those who stress what one might call the more spectacular gifts of Spirit—tongues, prophecies, miracles, and so forth. And on the other hand, there have always been those whose stress was on the quieter things which help to build up the unity of fellowship—love, joy, peace, and so forth.

The place where this is most fully worked out in the New Testament is in Paul's first letter to the Corinthians. Evidently the Corinthians were troubled about this question of the gift of the Spirit, and they asked Paul to tell them which is the greatest gift. Paul answered in the long passage which you find in the twelfth, thirteenth and fourteenth chapters of First Corinthians.

First of all he gives them the criterion, the basic test:

> About gifts of the Spirit, there are some things of which I do not wish you to remain ignorant. You know how, in the days when you were still pagan, you were swept off to those dumb heathen gods, however you happened to be led. For

this reason I must impress upon you that no one who says 'A curse on Jesus!' can be speaking under the influence of the Spirit of God. And no one can say 'Jesus is Lord!' except under the influence of the Holy Spirit.

I Corinthians 12:1-3.

The basic criterion by which we may determine where the Spirit is, is the relationship to Jesus Christ. It is the confession that Jesus is Lord. It is the explicit confession that Jesus is the center of the community, that everything is owed to him.

Second, there is a great variety of differents gifts of the Spirit—one Spirit but many gifts. Just as the one rainfall that falls on the ground brings forth a great variety of different grasses and flowers and shrubs, so the one Spirit of God, given to men in all their great variety, is expressed in a great variety of gifts. Paul has at least four places where he gives a list of these gifts. So there was clearly no fixed catalog in his mind. Here he gives the following:

There are varieties of gifts, but the same Spirit. There are varieties of service, but the same Lord. There are many forms of work, but all of them, in all men, are the work of the same God. In each of us the Spirit is manifested in one particular way, for some useful purpose. One man, through the Spirit, has the gift of wise speech, while another, by the power of the same Spirit, can put the deepest knowledge into words. Another, by the same Spirit, is granted faith; another, by the one Spirit, gifts of healing and another miraculous powers; another has the gift of prophecy, and another ability to distinguish true spirits from false; yet another has the gift of ecstatic utterance of different kinds, and another the ability to interpret it. But all these gifts are the work of one and the same Spirit, distributing them separately to each individual at will.

I Corinthians 12:4-11.

But Paul goes on, in the famous metaphor of the body, to indicate the meaning of this variety. It is not a meaningless or purposeless variety. On the contrary, it is to be understood in terms of the variety of the different limbs in our body. We have eyes, a nose, ears, mouth, hands, feet. The whole point of these things is that they are different from one another. And their variety is necessary for the healthy growth of the body. Their variety is precisely what contributes to the unity of the body.

And, therefore, he says, it is absurd to have a competition among the different limbs as to which is the most important. Or even more absurd to say that all should be the same. He has a very amusing passage that pictures the ear looking at the nose and saying, "You are not an ear, you don't belong to me; we evidently are of different families. You can go your way and I will go mine." And Paul asks: "What would be the use if the body was all ears? or all noses?" A basket full of noses is no good as a body.

But this is exactly what a great many Christians want to have. They want to have a party made up of people who are exactly the same, who talk the same language, who make the same noises, who are excited about the same things; a basket full of noses, a box full of ears. This is not a body. The whole point, says Paul, is that the variety is given for the sake of unity, for the sake of building up the body in health.

And then he comes round again to his list. But this time he has a different list. "Are all apostles? all prophets? all teachers? Do all work miracles? Have all the gifts of healing? Do all speak in tongues? Can all interpret them?" Of course not? there is a great variety. And so, which is the most important of these gifts? Paul's answer is:

> I may speak in tongues of men or of angels, but if I am without love, I am a sounding gong or a clanging cymbal. I may have the gift of prophecy, and know every hidden truth; I may have faith strong enough to move mountains; but if I have no love, I am nothing. I may dole out all I possess, or even give my body to be burnt, but if I have no love, I am none the better.
>
> Love is patient; love is kind and envies no one. Love is never boastful, nor conceited, nor rude; never selfish, not quick to take offence. Love keeps no score of wrongs; does not gloat over other men's sins, but delights in the truth. There is nothing love cannot face; there is no limit to its faith, its hope, and its endurance.
>
> Love will never come to an end. Are there prophets? their work will be over. Are there tongues of ecstasy? they will cease. Is there

knowledge? it will vanish away; for our knowledge and our prophecy alike are partial, and the partial vanishes when wholeness comes.

I Corinthians 13:1-9.

Which is the greatest gift? Which is the most important limb in the body? Can you make a hierarchy among the limbs? If you want an answer to that question, I can give it to you. Consider your hand. It is very useful to you, and you cannot get on without it. But if you took a tourniquet and put it around your arm and screwed it tight enough, and left it for a week, you would still have a hand, but it would be no use to you. Unless blood is circulating through your body, none of the limbs is of any good. Which, then, is the most important? It is that which keeps the whole body together, that which makes it possible for each of the different limbs to minister as it can to the whole body. The greatest gift of the Spirit is the love that binds all together.

And so Paul comes back to the original question.

Put love first, but there are other gifts of the Spirit at which you should aim also, and above all prophecy. When a man is using the language of ecstasy he is talking with God, not with men, for no man understands him; he is no doubt inspired, but he speaks mysteries. On the other hand, when a man prophesies, he is talking to men, and his words have power to build; they stimulate and they encourage. The language of ecstasy is good for the speaker himself, but it is prophecy that builds up a Christian community. I should be pleased for you all to use the tongues of ecstasy, but better pleased for you to prophesy. The prophet is worth more than the man of ecstatic speech—unless indeed he can explain its meaning, and so help to build up the community. . . .

Thank God, I am more gifted in ecstatic utterance than any of you, but in the congregation I would rather speak five intelligible words, for the benefit of others as well as myself, than thousands of words in the language of ecstasy.

I Corinthians 14:1-5, 18-19.

The gifts which are most to be prized are those which build up the fellowship. Paul does not despise the gift of tongues. He includes it in all his lists, although he always puts it at the bottom. He himself says that he speaks in tongues. And he very specifically explains what is the value of it (and this has been confirmed by many friends of mine who have the gift of tongues), namely, that it is a way of speaking to God. It is a liberation of the tongue to speak with the utmost freedom to God. Good. Let us thank God for it. Paul does not despise it. But, he says, it is more important to develop those gifts which build up the fellowship. And therefore, after the passage which we have just read, he has a rather sharp sentence: Thank God that I am more gifted in tongues than any of you, but in the congregation I would rather speak five intelligible words for the benefit of others, than ten thousand words in a tongue.

That is a very straight remark. Some Christians seem to think that if one can speak ten thousand words per minute, then one is definitely all right. Paul says that he would rather speak five words with intelligence which other people could understand than ten thousand words in a tongue. The essential point is that this life of the Spirit is the life of a community. Therefore, those gifts of the Spirit which we are above all to seek are those which build up the fellowship. The essential mark of the new life in the Spirit is that it is a common life, which usually come in the latter part of his letters, towards a goal that is before all of us.

If you look at Paul's descriptions of the Christian life, which usually come in the latter part of his letters, you will see that every single one of them is in terms of the life of a community. You will never find Paul describing an ideal Christian man. Such a thing would be a monstrosity to him. He would never have thought of it. There is no such thing as an ideal Christian man or woman. There is only an ideal Christian fellowship, an ideal community. And everything that Paul says about the Christian life is said about the fellowship and about our mutual relationship within our fellowship. Look at Galatians 5 and 6, Ephesians 5, Colossians 3. This new life, if I may put it so, is caught and lived within a fellowship. There are very different gifts. But they are to be used to help one another. Never am I to envy another person because he has gifts that I do not have. Never am I to feel vexed because someone else can speak in tongues, or can prophesy, or perform miracles, or has gifts of leadership, or gifts of wisdom that I do not have. The Holy Spirit has given some gift to everyone and that is the gift that we are to use in building up the body in health. In other words, we should rejoice in the differences between us, rejoice precisely in those things in which we are different from one another.

In this letter to the Corinthians, Paul had to deal with this question of tongues at some length, apparently because this was one of the things which worried them. But in many other places where he speaks about the Spirit, he does not mention tongues at all. As far as I can remember, there is no other place in Paul's writing where he speaks about the gift of tongues. The greatest passage of all his writings dealing with life in the Spirit is Romans 8. And with that I would like to finish. In that great chapter Paul uses three key words to describe what it means to live in the community of the Spirit. They are the words *freedom, sonship,* and *hope.*

First of all, at the beginning of the chapter, he speaks of how Christ has set us free. There is no condemnation for those who are united with Christ Jesus, because in Christ Jesus the life-giving law of the Spirit has set you free from the law of sin and death. What the law could never do, because our flesh robs it of power, God has done by sending his own son, in a form like that of our own sinful flesh and as a sacrifice for sin. He has passed judgment against sin within that very nature, so that the commandment of the law may find fulfilment in us whose conduct is no longer under the control of the flesh but of the Spirit. Freedom from sin, freedom from death, freedom from the law— this is what Christ has given to us through the Spirit.

Saul as a Pharisee, as a Jew, had been a slave. It would have been shocking to him if anyone had said that to him at that time, but now he believed that it was true. All his piety, all his devotion, all his passionate religious activity, were kinds of slavery. He was a slave of the law. More precisely, he was the slave of his own compulsive need to prove that he was a righteous and godly person. Like many people in all religions—and not least in Christianity—he was bound by rules and regulations, some inspired by religion, some self-imposed. It was impossible for him simply to be a free man—as Jesus was a free man—doing the loving thing, the right thing, spontaneously from his heart. He was a slave under the law.

His new relationship with Christ had set him free. Now that he had given up the hopeless attempt to be a good man, now that his defenses were down, he had nothing to do but express his thankfulness to Jesus, who loved him and died for him. And so, because his defenses were down, the Spirit of Jesus could come in and make life what it was meant by God to be—a continuous, spontaneous, willing offering of love and obedience to the giver of all. That theme of freedom from the law is worked out fully and dramatically in his Epistle to the Galatians.

Second, Paul says life in the Spirit means sonship.

> For all who are moved by the Spirit of God are sons of God. The Spirit you have received is not a spirit of slavery leading you back into a life of fear, but a Spirit that makes us sons, enabling us to cry 'Abba! Father!' In that cry the Spirit of

> God joins with our spirit in testifying that we are
> God's children; and if children, then heirs.
>
> Romans 8:14-16.

The same Spirit that was in Jesus fills our hearts and finds expression in the same word that was on the lips of Jesus: Abba, My Father. This means the same attitude that Jesus had in every situation, an attitude of trustful loving obedience, an absolute assurance that everything we do and everything that is done to us, in every circumstance, can be simply offered up into the Father's hands with the assurance that—however dark the hour—all will be well. It is the attitude of Jesus on the cross, sustained through all the experiences of life right up to and including the final experience of death: "Father, into thy hands I commend my spirit." The Spirit is the Spirit of sonship.

Third, the life in the Spirit means hope. Immediately following the passage we just read, Paul goes on to say this :

> In that cry the Spirit of God joins with our spirit
> in testifying that we are God's children; and if
> children, then heirs. We are God's heirs and
> Christ's fellow-heirs, if we share his sufferings
> now in order to share his splendour hereafter.

Life in the Spirit means hope. If we are sons, then we are heirs, and we can look forward eagerly and confidently, but also patiently, to coming into our Father's estate. We are nothing now. We are not the owners of all things—very much the reverse. But the

secret of the future belongs to us. We are the heirs of
God's kingdom. And, therefore, we are always looking
forward, full of hope.

The same idea is expressed by Paul in another way
when he speaks of the Holy Spirit as the earnest of our
inheritance. The Greek word is *arrabon.* It is a commer-
cial word, which simply means cash in advance. If you
have to pay a thousand dollars, and you give the man a
hundred dollars as cash in advance, it is called in Greek
arrabon. That is the word that Paul used for the Holy
Spirit in several of his letters. It is as it were the
advance payment, and therefore the guarantee of our
inheritance. It is as though our Father was giving us
now an advance instalment of the estate to which we
are heirs. And this means that we are both happy for
what we have received and also hopeful for what is still
to come.

This is one of the great things of this wonderful
chapter—that it expresses the balance in the Christian
life between what we have received and what we still
long for. "We have been saved, though only in hope.
Now to see is no longer to hope. Why should a man
endure and wait for what he already sees. But if we
hope for something we do not yet see, then in waiting
for it we show our endurance." There is a balance in
the Christian life. We have received something more
precious than words can describe, and yet it is only a
foretaste, it is only an *arrabon,* it is only an advance
payment, it is only something which assures us of what
is to come, and helps us to wait for it patiently.

In these chapters I am trying to convey my faith
that in Jesus Christ we are given the direction for our

lives, which is also the direction in which God intends to lead the whole creation, and which, therefore, can give meaning to our individual lives. But now we have come to a crucial point in the argument. We have seen first that the cross and resurrection of Jesus constitute a turning point, a point at which we are stopped in our tracks and sent off in a new direction. And we have seen, second, that this direction is towards a community of free people who, being freed from bondage to law, to sin, and to death, are open to God's Spirit and are thereby enabled to live together in life built up in mutual love and responsibility.

And third, we have seen that a foretaste of that life of freedom in community is given to us now. We do not just long for it and hope for it and strive for it and wait for it; we also have a foretaste of it now, a foretaste that makes us sure that we are going in the right direction.

This leads to the final point. In a twilight world where people are lost and asking their way, a few people marching together in one direction with the light of hope and expectation on their faces will surely prompt others to ask: "Where are you going?" If the Holy Spirit is the foretaste of what is to come, that will explain why it is that the New Testament often speaks of the function of the Holy Spirit as witness. "When the Holy Spirit comes to you, you will be my witnesses." That is a promise, not a command. He did not say, "you must be my witnesses." He said, "when the Holy Spirit comes to you, you will be my witnesses." So it is also in other passages in the Gospels, "When the Holy Spirit comes, he will bear witness for me, and you also will be my witnesses." If I may return to the metaphor with which I began, it is not just that we have a compass. We have much more than that. We have a foretaste of the joy for which the world and all men were made. It is that foretaste which prompts men to ask, "Where are you going? What is the secret of your hope?"

That hope is hope not just for us but for the whole world. We have no right to keep it to ourselves. To answer the question, "What is the hope for the world?", will be our next task.

Hope for the World

The word hope is one of the key words in the Christian religion. In this respect Christianity parts company, for example, with the main tradition of Indian religion and philosophy. Indian wisdom has generally advised man that it is better to be content with what he has and not to follow the vain delusions of hope which in the end are bound to disappoint him. If there is a hope, according to this tradition, it is rather to be found in escape from this world, from the grip of our karma and the endless cycle of rebirth.

But even if we look at our ordinary use in the languages which we speak, I think that one has to say that what the Bible says about hope is only very faintly reflected in our languages. In Tamil, the word *nambukirain,* which is used for hope, really means simply, "I think." The effect of that can be seen when Tamil is translated back into English. I once had a letter from a friend whose English was not very good, which began, "I hope that you are having a bad fever." It is clear that what he really meant was, "I think you are having a bad fever." If you were to take a statistical analysis of all the occurrences of the word hope in the English language, undoubtedly the great majority of occurrences would be in the sentence, "I hope it doesn't rain tomorrow." It almost always does rain. The word hope, in other words, merely expresses a desire which may or may not be fulfilled.

By contrast, when the Bible speaks of hope, along with faith and love, as one of the three enduring realities on which our life in Jesus Christ is based, it means something much stronger than that. Hope in the Bible is an eager and patient waiting for something which is good, and something which is sure because God has promised it.

I want to spend a moment with this word *promise,* because it is fundamental to our understanding of what the Bible has to say about hope. In the Bible, hope for the future is not the result of what can be calculated as the probable result of present trends. It is not an extrapolation of our present experience. It is not analogous to the now popular science of futurology. From the beginning of the Bible we see God revealing himself to men as one who promises good things, things which are not yet seen, but which are hoped for on the basis of his promise. They are things, moreover, which are not merely hoped for but are actually reached after, because God not only promises good things but he also invites men to trust his promises and to set out in the direction of the good things which he promises.

This becomes very clear in the story near the beginning of the Bible which marks the beginning of the story of salvation. Abraham, living in the land of Har-

ran, is invited to leave his home and his kindred and set
out for an unknown land, simply trusting in God's
promise: "I will make you a great nation, and in you
all the nations of the earth shall bless themselves."
Abraham becomes the father of the faithful, according
to the Bible—the archetype of those who trust God's
promises, and who are willing to set out in pursuit of
them.

In other words, in the Bible, the world as it is, is not
the ground of our hope and cannot be. The fact is, as
we already saw, that the world as it is, is rather the
object of our protest than the ground of our hope.
Hope is grounded in what God intends and what he has
promised. And in the strength of that promise men can
dare to say No to the world as it is, to be skeptics
regarding what now is, to refuse to be controlled by
present experience, to resist the world to the point of
death—as Jesus did—trusting in the as-yet-unseen promises of God. That is the basis of the biblical picture of
hope.

But what has God promised? What are we justified
in hoping for?

If one listened to a good deal of the language of
popular Christianity of the present day, one would get
the impression that what I have to hope for is simply
that I, and perhaps some of my friends, will escape
from hell and get to heaven. In other words, what is
often presented as the Christian hope is a purely selfish
hope for my own safety and happiness to be attained
essentially by escaping out of this world into another.

It is not difficult to see how this has become so
popular in the Indian Church today, because it is

almost identical with the Hindu idea of salvation as escape from the world of *maya*. It also is perhaps something that corresponds unfortunately with the idea of Christianity that has been developed under the shadow of Western missions. The idea is that becoming a Christian (forgive me if I put it crudely) means becoming a shareholder in a mutual benefit society in which the members are entitled to educational, medical, and social facilities free of cost.

When we turn to the Bible, we find that the reality is very different. If one may put the contrast as sharply as possible, the great emphasis in the biblical statement of what God has promised is not that I am going to escape out of this world into another, but that Christ is coming back to this world to reign. I am putting it sharply, but not, I think, improperly. It is impossible to doubt that this is the main emphasis in what the Bible teaches about the future. In the Old Testament, the great prophecies of the messianic kingdom speak of something on the earth. Certainly it is a transformed and renewed earth, where the wilderness blossoms like the rose, and there are streams in the desert, and the lion and the lamb feed together—but still it is of this world that we are thinking. And even at the very end of the New Testament where we are given the vision of the new Jerusalem, the holy city, it does not remain in heaven but comes down out of heaven.

The promise of God in the Bible is centered in the coming of his reign, his kingdom, and the doing of his will on earth, as it is in heaven. That is what we are authorized by our Lord himself to pray for and to hope for.

But what exactly does this entitle us to hope for?

This question has been answered in different ways during the nineteen centuries of church history.

There have been, from time to time, groups of Christians who took as their clue the passage in the book of Revelation describing the thousand-year reign of Christ and the saints on earth before the final judgment, the so-called millennium. These millenarian groups, as they have been called, have usually identified some particular political order which they were working for as the promised millennium. Think, for example, of some of the men in Cromwell's army. These hopes have always been disappointed, and the millenarians have always been on the fringe of the church. And yet they have unquestionably borne witness to one central element in the whole biblical faith.

In the eighteenth century another form of this belief arose in Europe under the name of the doctrine of progress. The French and German philosophers of the Enlightenment, who paved the way for the French Revolution, believed that mankind had discovered the secret of perpetual progress and that one could therefore look forward to an unlimited advance of knowledge and technical skill until mankind would live together in a state of permanent wisdom, comfort, and peace.

No one can deny that some of the hopes of these philosophers have been realized. The advance in knowledge and technical skill in the past two hundred years has been far beyond their wildest dreams, and it continues with accelerating pace. But no one can say that wisdom has increased or that peace is more secure.

Today the doctrine of progress in its classical form is probably believed by hardly anyone. We have instead the new and growing science of futurology, to which some of the best scientists in such prestigious institutions as MIT and the Rand Corporation are devoting themselves. Futurology is the study of the future by examination and extrapolation from the present. The object is not to make any judgment about what is desirable but only to make an intelligent forecast of what is probable on the basis of existing facts and trends.

Probably most of us who have studied the literature of the futurologists will agree with Winston Churchill, who on being presented with one of their reports said, "I shall be very content to be dead before this happens." But even if we have to look forward not to the nightmares of the futurologist but to the dreams of peace and happiness of the French philosophers, the point is still the same: I shall be dead before this happens. What, then, does all this have to do with me, or with anyone who has to live his life, do his work and die his death, now, as a human person? Does this person who happens to be me, who may be really very unimportant but who seems very important to me, does this living human person—whether it is I or you— have any real place either in the dreams of the philosophers or in the reports of the futurologists? Or am I just a cog, a small cog in the machine? If that is so—what meaning is there in my life? Even if the machine is going somewhere worthwhile, I am not. I shall be out of the picture before that day comes.

This protest on behalf of the individual human person cannot be ignored. In the name of God, if we are Christians, we would have to assert that every human soul is precious in the sight of God; that he cannot be treated merely as expendable raw material for the programs of the philosophers or the technologists; and that he has a dignity and a destiny which is more, infinitely more, than simply his particular contribution to social and technical progress. Man has an eternal destiny.

So the Christian faith has always asserted. Ancient Judaism did not have that faith. It did not believe in any significant or worthwhile life after death. But based on the resurrection of Jesus, Christians have always believed in and hoped for some kind of personal future beyond the grave.

How can this be reconciled with belief in a real meaning in human history on this earth? If my life is really directed towards a future life beyond death, why should I care about the future of this world? And what in any case does the future of this world mean for me?

In the little book by Teilhard de Chardin called *The Divine Milieu* there is a sharp criticism of Christianity put into the mouth of an agnostic scientist. One could not read that without feeling that these must be the words of some actual scientist who had addressed them to Teilhard himself. What this agnostic scientist said was this: "You Christians who engage in scientific activities are not serious. You are only playing at it. It does not really matter to you whether your experiments succeed or not, whether the truth is established or not. From your point of view the only thing that matters is that you go to heaven at the end. In other words, you may be honest and painstaking and sincere in your work, but what finally happens afterwards does not matter to you. You are, therefore, only playing at science and it would be better for you to keep out of it altogether and leave it to people who are serious about it."

Is that a just criticism? Does it really matter to us? Does it really matter to God whether our work endures and makes a solid contribution to the welfare of this world? Or do we think that since the world is going to be destroyed anyway, the only thing that matters is that our work should be sincere and honest so that we will pass the test and receive our reward?

One may put it in the form of an illustration. A student of engineering is called upon to make a design for a bridge as an examination exercise. If he does his calculation wrong, the worst that happens is that he fails to get his degree. But if he is an engineer working for the Department of Public Works and he makes the same mistake, a lot of people are liable to get killed.

What is our situation in this world? Does anything serious result from what we do, except that we either pass or fail in the examination?

What, again, are we authorized to hope for? What has God promised? To answer these questions, we must go back again to the center from which I have been suggesting our direction can be taken—the cross and resurrection of Jesus. How do we understand the promises of God in the light of the cross and the resurrection of Jesus?

The first point is that death has no longer the last word. The dilemma with which we have been wrestling, namely that we do not seem to be able to find meaning at the same time both for the life of the individual person and for the history of the world, this dilemma rests upon the fact that death removes the individual from world history before history has reached its goal. There are therefore, apparently, different goals for the individual and for the human race as a whole. If death has the last word, there is no resolution of that problem; they must remain different to the end.

At Easter we know that death does not have the last word. The death of Jesus was—from one point of view—the failure of his mission. Israel did not repent and believe. The movement he had sought to launch as a historical movement came to an end in the agony and shame of Calvary. But this defeat was turned into victory.

And yet we must say again, this does not mean that defeat was obliterated. Death was not obliterated. The victory is the victory of the crucified. The risen Lord bears the wounds of the nails and the spear on his body. The message of victory continues to have the cross at its center. Jesus goes from his baptism in the Jordan to his resurrection and ascension and the discipling of all the nations, and the gathering of all peoples into the Kingdom of God, down through the valley of death by way of the cross. There is no other way. There is no bypass. The way goes down into the valley of death and there is no bridge over the valley— either for Jesus or for those who come after him. That is the first point.

Second, what is seen in the experience of Jesus and his faithful followers is, according to the New Testament, written large across the history of the world, that history which is imaginatively sketched for us in what we call the apocalyptic passages of the New Testament, for example the thirteenth chapter of

Mark. There is the assurance of victory. Death is conquered. But the way to that victorious end goes through conflict and suffering, wars and rumors of wars, false Messiahs, antichrist, the blood of martyrs, and even the shaking of the physical universe. There is a road which leads through world history to the Kingdom of God, but it is a road which goes down through the valley of death and there is no bridge. The powers of evil have to be overcome in this world through the voluntary suffering of Christ and his people.

Third, in the fifteenth chapter of Corinthians Paul gives his fullest connected account of the meaning of the resurrection for human history. He begins by reminding his readers of all the witnesses who can testify to the reality of the resurrection. Then in the crucial paragraph he sketches the prospect that is opened up by the resurrection:

> If it is for this life only that Christ has given us hope, we of all men are most to be pitied.
> But the truth is, Christ was raised to life—the first-fruits of the harvest of the dead. For since it was a man who brought death into the world, a man also brought resurrection of the dead. As in Adam all men die, so in Christ all will be brought to life; but each in his own proper place: Christ the first-fruits, and afterwards, at his coming, those who belong to Christ. Then comes the end, when he delivers up the kingdom to God the father, after abolishing every kind of domination, authority, and power.

I Corinthians 15:19-25.

We note here that in this sketch there are several stages in the working out of the consequences of the resurrection. First Christ himself, the given fact which is the beginning of it all. Then those who belong to Christ, those who have been made the people of Christ. But then there is a struggle until all things, the whole universe, is brought under obedience to Christ. This does not happen immediately. There is the indication of a period, perhaps a long period, before all things are subjected to Christ. Finally the rule is delivered to God the Father who is supreme over all.

There are three things to notice in this.

First, the story does not stop with the resurrection of those who belong to Christ. A great many Christians speak as though it did, as though the only meaning of the resurrection is hope for the resurrection of Christians, of those who believe in Christ. This is only part of the story. The matter does not end until all things—the universe—have been brought under the control of Christ.

Second, there is a period of struggle before all enemies are subdued. This is the period which may be described, on the basis of this paragraph, as the period of the Kingdom of Christ, still battling with the enemies of God.

Third, the question is raised in the latter part of the chapter about the continuity between this life that we know and the life to come. Is it the same or is it different? This question is answered by means of a parable. Paul uses the parable that Jesus himself had used. He says it is like the grain that falls into the ground. It disappears and is lost. You search for it but you won't find it. But, out of that loss, that disappearance, a new thing, a greater and more glorious thing, is created. In other words there is both discontinuity and continuity. There is a real death. We must die. Our works perish. The world itself decays. To use the parable I used before, there is no bridge, there is no bypass. But the resources of God are great enough to raise up, out of that which is committed to him in death, something more glorious, more full of life.

Finally, we turn to the eighth chapter of Romans. There Paul gives us another picture of the hope which is the result of Christ's death and resurrection. He uses a different metaphor, not that of the germination of a seed, but that of childbirth. We saw how the result of Christ's death and resurrection is a new life in the Spirit marked by freedom, sonship, and hope. And now as this chapter proceeds, Paul goes on to spell out that hope more fully. It begins with the renewal of our own personal lives:

> Moreover, if the Spirit of him who raised Jesus from the dead dwells within you, then the God who raised Christ Jesus from the dead will also give new life to your mortal bodies through his indwelling Spirit.
>
> Romans 8:11.

This is the beginning, the renewal of our whole personality. The God who raised Jesus from the dead is able to quicken us. But it does not stop there. We see the same pattern as in the fifteenth chapter of I Corinthians. The renewal extends to the whole created universe.

> For the created universe waits with eager expectation for God's sons to be revealed. It was made the victim of frustration, not by its own choice, but because of him who made it so; yet always there was hope, because the universe itself is to be free from the shackles of mortality and enter upon the liberty and splendour of the children of God. Up to the present, we know, the whole created universe groans in all its parts as if in the pangs of childbirth. Not only so, but even we, to whom the Spirit is given as firstfruits of the harvest to come, are groaning inwardly while we wait for God to make us his sons and set our whole body free. For we have been saved, though only in hope. Now to see is no longer to hope; why should man endure and wait for what he already sees? But if we hope for something we do not yet see, then, in waiting for it, we show our endurance.

> Romans 8:19-25.

The world is in pain, and we ourselves are in pain. But it is not a meaningless pain. It is the pain of childbirth. A new creation, a new world is coming to birth, a world which will be the world of God's redeemed and free children. We share in the pangs of childbirth of this new creation. What lies ahead of us, the thing we hope for, is not just our personal renewal but the renewal of the whole cosmos, the whole creation, so that it may no longer be the world of frustration, but be the reflection and instrument of God's glory.

In the third chapter of I Corinthians, there is a short passage which is also very relevant to our theme, because it deals with the question of our work. It concerns the future not only of ourselves but of our work, the question with which Teilhard de Chardin was wrestling in that passage which I quoted.

> Or again, you are God's building. I am like a skilled master-builder who by God's grace laid the foundation, and someone else is putting up the building. Let each take care how he builds. There can be no other foundation beyond that which is already laid: I mean Jesus Christ himself. If any one builds on that foundation with gold, silver, and fine stone, or with wood, hay, and straw, the work that each man does will at last be brought to light; the day of Judgement will expose it. For that day dawns in fire, and the fire will test the worth of each man's work. If a man's building stands, he will be rewarded; if it burns, he will have to bear the loss; and yet he will escape with his life, as one might from fire.
> I Corinthians 3:10-15.

Here there is a third metaphor, the metaphor of fire. All things must pass through fire, a purifying fire, a fire which will destroy that which is unfit to endure. Some of our work will be destroyed; some of it, by God's grace, may pass the test. The point is that it is not just that we ourselves hope for a personal future. It is that we hope that what we have done—the part we have played in the building of the new order whose foundation is Jesus Christ—may come through that fire cleansed and fit for a place in God's new city.

Finally we come to the Book of Revelation, the last book of the Bible, where we have the fullest and most wonderful picture, painted by a Christian prophet, of the meaning of history and of the things for which we can hope. Let me mention a few very simple points, key points, of this great interpretation of the promises of God.

We begin with the scroll sealed with seven seals. History is a secret. Even the futurologists cannot tell us with certainty what is to happen. We cannot ourselves break the seals to open the scroll and unveil the secret. Who can do that? Who has the clue to history? Who can break the seal and open the book? The answer is this. Standing between the throne of God and the created world, there is a lamb, slain. He alone can provide the clue, Jesus the crucified. He alone can break the seals and open the book.

Then when the seals are broken and the book is opened, history is revealed to us as a scene of frightful conflict. The key to this conflict is that the obscene powers that rule the world, the monster who rules all the peoples, the harlot who seduces them, and the false prophet who deludes them with his propaganda—these are to be destroyed. John in his writing makes it clear what he has in mind. He meant the vast military power of the Roman Empire, with its claim to divinity and eternity, with its vast apparatus of propaganda and with its attendant economic power which could seduce all the nations of the earth and bring them into the net of its all-devouring commerce. The monster and the harlot and the prophet are enduring features of the human scene. Political, military, and economic power, and the power of propaganda have become much greater and more formidable than in the days when John wrote his book.

How will these powers be destroyed? What is the force, the mighty power, that can destroy them? They can be destroyed only by the blood of the lamb and of his followers. Their clothes are soaked in blood, as his are also soaked in blood, before the battle begins. It is not the blood of Jesus' enemies; it is his own blood that wins the victory. And those who follow him, sharing his suffering and his testimony, follow him wherever he goes. It is by their faithfulness to death that the frightful powers of evil are overcome.

The fourth point to be noted is that their victory is, first of all, a victory on this earth. John is speaking about the things that are shortly to be. He is speaking about things which were indeed to happen within a few years of his writing of his book. John is speaking of something which is to happen on this earth, and he expresses it by means of the picture of the thousand-year reign of Christ and his martyred followers. This is the consummation of that reign of Jesus which began at his resurrection and ascension. "He must reign until all enemies are put under his feet." It is the consummation of that long struggle of which Paul speaks in the fifteenth chapter of I Corinthians. These chosen followers who have been made kings and priests will reign with him over the nations.

But, fifth, the resources of evil are still not yet exhausted. Even the millennium does not completely remove them, nor is it immune from the attack of evil. The mysterious forces of Gog and Magog, the ultimate resources of evil beyond everything that we can imagine, are still held in reserve. And the final overthrow of evil is wholly the work of God.

And now comes the judgment, the judgment of all the nations, when not only the record of men's deeds is brought forward, not only the deeds, good and evil, that men have done in their lives, are finally brought to light, but also the Lamb's Book of Life wherein are written the names of those to whom he has been pleased to give the gift of life. Now only death and hell are destroyed, and now also those who have finally refused the Lamb's gift of life are destroyed.

And then comes the vision that is the consummation of it all, the New Jerusalem, the holy city coming down from heaven as a bride adorned for her husband. Not the harlot city of Rome which sucked into itself all the wealth of the nations, but the Holy City whose builder and maker is God. Into that city nothing unclean may enter, but—and this is truly the most remarkable thing in the whole book—the nations walk by its light and the kings of the earth bring into it their treasures. Remember that the nations are the heathen nations, the Gentiles, those who had trampled the Holy City at the end of the millennium. And the kings of the earth are the kings of these pagan nations. It is still a city on earth, but a wholly renewed earth. It is a city, not a church, not even a conference center, but a city, in other words, it is the end of the long story of man's civilization. The nations (in the language of the New Testament that means the Gentiles, the heathen nations) walk in its light, and their kings bring their treasures into it. Nothing, in other words, of human labor, human culture, human learning, nothing that goes to make up what we call human civilization, is excluded from a place in God's city, except that which is unclean, that which is incompatible with who and what God is.

Now indeed the long story of creation reaches its consummation. When God made the world he pronounced it very good, but he also called upon man to till the ground and cultivate it, to be his co-worker in completing the work of creation, and making the earth what he wanted it to be. Man's work of creation has indeed been gigantic, changing the face of the earth; but it has been monstrous, often an obscene caricature of what God intended, as the city of Rome was an obscene parody of the City of God. But God has not given up and will not give up until his work is finished, until all that is unclean, all that is a caricature of what God intends, is destroyed, and there stands the City of God which is both the consummation of all men's corporate labors throughout the history of civilization, and also the consummation of each man's personal history. For there in the midst of the streets of the City the servants of the Lamb will see him face to face and worship him and bear his name on their foreheads.

But who are these servants of the Lamb? What is this committed fellowship of those who are called upon to share with the Lamb in the battles and the agonies of history?

That is to be our next subject.

5

A Committed People

If you have read the famous little red book of Chairman Mao, you will know that among its very first sentences is this: "If you want to have a revolution, the first necessity is to have a strong Communist Party."

Ideas change the world only if there are people committed to those ideas, organized to work together for their realization.

If God is leading the world in the direction indicated by the cross and resurrection of Christ Jesus, where is the body of committed people who are ready to go that way and to take the rest of mankind with them?

In the Book of Revelation we read of the army of men, ransomed from all mankind to be the firstfruits for God and for Jesus, who "follow the Lamb wherever he goes" (Rev. 14:4). In the vision of John, though Jesus died alone on the cross, he does not fight the battle of history alone. He has his picked and consecrated army who go with him through all the conflict, and their robes, like his, are soaked in blood—his blood.

This is only one of the many ways in which the Bible presents to us the picture of a people committed to God and to his Kingdom. In the Old Testament, Israel is called to be such a people, not just for their own blessing, but for the blessing of the nations. They are to be a kingdom of priests for God, to mediate both his rule and his forgiveness to all the nations. They are to be witnesses to the nations who do not know God. They are to be a light to the nations and the bearers of salvation to the ends of the earth.

But Israel persistently misunderstood what it meant to be God's committed people. Persistently they misinterpreted it as a special privilege for themselves rather than a special responsibility towards the other nations of the world. Prophet after prophet attacked this fatal introversion. Among the most precious gems of the Old Testament prophecy is the story of Jonah. It is a vivid picture of Israel stubbornly refusing to obey God's call to bring the message of salvation to the pagan empire of Assyria, and finally ending in a fit of sulky self-pity when the pagan empire begins to repent and turn to God.

In the same way Jesus accuses the religious teachers of his time of keeping to themselves the treasure that was given for all men. They have done the stupidest possible thing: they have hidden the light under a barrel; they have buried their treasure in a napkin in the ground; they have barred and bolted the Kingdom of heaven against men who would have come in.

And in the same way—alas—the Christian church has

been guilty through the centuries of the same fatal introversion. What was given as a mission to the world has been twisted into a privilege for ourselves. We have been more concerned that the church should be big and prosperous and strong than that God's will should be done in the world. We have sought our own aggrandizement rather than the fulfilment of the task for which we were called. Look at John's picture of the 144,000 who follow the Lamb wherever he goes and put it alongside a picture of the Christian church today. How often is the Christian church no more than a self-centered community only faintly concerned that God's will be done in the life of the world, only faintly interested in justice and mercy for this earth's exploited masses, but passionately devoted to our own protection and advancement as a community and, if we are piously inclined, to assuring that after a comfortable passage through this life we can look forward to a guaranteed place in the foam-rubber-padded seats of heaven.

How is it that we have so terribly misunderstood our Lord's intention? I want to answer that question by grasping what is, I think, the central point: the point at which the meaning of church membership is clear, baptism. To understand what baptism is, we must begin where all our four Gospels begin—with the baptism of John. All the records agree that that is where the gospel concerning Jesus begins. John was a prophet in the true tradition of Old Testament prophecy—in the tradition of Elijah, Amos, Isaiah, and Jeremiah. He came, as they had done in their days, to bring God's word to his people, to warn them of the approaching day of judgment and to call them to repent and change their way of life. In this he was not different from the earlier prophets.

The Old Testament prophets had often supported their words by symbolic actions. Jeremiah went and buried his belt near the Euphrates as a sign of what was going to happen to the people of Jerusalem. Zedekiah, son of Kenaanah, made iron bows and said to King Ahab, "with these you will gore the Syrians." Isaiah and Ezekiel also used visible signs to bring home their message.

John did the same. He used the sign of washing, to say as vividly as possible to the people of Israel: "You are an unclean people. Only if someone washes you will you be fit to meet your God."

The authorized leaders in Israel stood aloof from John and his baptism. They did not think that they needed any cleansing beyond what the Law already provided. But thousands of ordinary men and women, moved by a deep sense of need, came, heard and were baptized.

Among them came one whom John already knew, for he was a kinsman. Why did Jesus come to be baptized? He had lived from his boyhood in that loving and trustful obedience to his Father which he expressed uniquely in the word *Abba*. He loved his Father and longed that his name should be hallowed and his Kingdom come and his will be done. He saw in the great movement of repentance and cleansing a work of his own Father. He longed to be part of that work, to be utterly identified with these men and women, burdened by sin and longing for cleansing. He came and stood before John as one among that crowd of sin-burdened men and women—a candidate for baptism.

We read in Mathew's Gospel that John would have stopped him, but Jesus answered: "Let it be so now, for thus it is fitting for us to fulfil all righteousness." At this point the true righteousness, the righteousness of God, as distinct from the righteousness of the Pharisees, is coming to light. As Paul was to say later: "He who knew no sin was made to be sin on our behalf, that we might become the righteousness of God in him." The sinless Son of God received the baptism of repentance for the remission of sin, making himself one with sinful men and taking upon himself the burden of our sin.

At that moment John's baptism was fulfilled. The baptism of the Spirit to which John had pointed was given to Jesus. The sign—baptism in water—was met by the thing which it signified—baptism in the Spirit. This was baptism not by water alone but by water and the Spirit. It was the beginning of the ministry and mission of the Messiah.

But it was only the beginning. What was begun at the Jordan River when Jesus identified himself totally with sinful men, was completed on Calvary when he bore on his own soul and body the whole appalling weight of the karma of humanity. When he himself spoke of this he spoke of it as the completion of his baptism. "I have a baptism to be baptized with, and how I am constrained until it is accomplished." Accomplished it was on the cross, and the same word is used here as he used in the final cry of triumph at the end: "It is finished—accomplished." The baptism of Jesus, begun at the Jordan River, was finished on the hill of Calvary.

But here is the next crucial point: it is not his baptism alone. He invited his disciples to share his baptism, even though they did not yet understand what it was. Remember the story of the two disciples who came to him asking for the chief places in heaven.

> James and John, the sons of Zebedee, approached him and said, 'Master, we should like you to do us a favour.' 'What is it you want me to do?' he asked. They answered, 'Grant us the right to sit in state with you, one at your right and the other at your left.' Jesus said to them, 'You do not understand what you are asking. Can you drink the cup that I drink, or be baptized with the baptism I am baptized with?' 'We can', they answered, Jesus said, 'The cup that I drink you shall drink, and the baptism I am baptized with shall be your baptism; but to sit at my right or left is not for me to grant; it is for those to whom it has already been assigned.'
>
> Mark 10:35-40.

"My cup you shall drink, and the baptism I am baptized with shall be your baptism"—that is his great promise to disciples who are still thinking not of Christ but of themselves, not of the travail of his soul, but of the security and safety and status of themselves. It is the same gracious promise and invitation that he gives to the disciples in the Upper Room, still quarreling about who is the greatest. "This is my body broken for you. This is my blood shed for you. Take, eat, and drink." My cup you shall drink and with my baptism you shall be baptized—from the baptism in water with which it begins through to its completion in taking up the cross and following me on the way of the cross.

This, then, is what Christian baptism is. It is the share that he graciously gives to us in his baptism, the baptism by which we are united with him in freely and gladly taking on himself the karma of humanity, united with him right up to the cross, united in the body broken and blood shed, in order that we may also be united with him in his risen life through the Spirit. Baptism means being enrolled among those who follow the Lamb wherever he goes. It is constantly renewed as we share his cup and are reunited with his dying and rising. It is completed in lives offered up to his service in the warfare of the Lamb with all the powers of evil.

Baptism has sometimes become a point of controversy because people come to it with the same attitude as James and John. They want only to be sure of safe seats in heaven for themselves. Thus baptism becomes a kind of life insurance policy, and there are plenty of private companies offering policies on competitive terms, second, third and fourth baptism, appealing all the time to the lowest elements of human nature—selfishness, cowardice and fear, exploiting what is basest in man. It is something by which the name of Christ is dishonored, and men in whom there is nobility of character will turn away from it in disgust. When our Lord said to his disciples, "Are you willing to be baptized with my baptism?" he was not offering them an extra immersion as a guarantee that their selfish ambitions would be fulfilled. He was asking whether they were willing to take up the cross and follow him through to the end. To accept that baptism means to accept the cross. Christ's committed people are those who follow the Lamb through the conflicts of history until that day when the powers of evil are finally destroyed.

What then should be the character of the committed people? In what ways does it serve God's Kingdom in this age? What will be its characteristic activities? I want to answer that question by suggesting five essential characteristics or activities of the church.

I would put this first: The church in the world will have the form of a servant. When Peter wanted to summarize the ministry of Jesus in a single phrase, he said that Jesus went about doing good. When John the Baptist doubted whether Jesus was the Messiah, Jesus answered by pointing to his works of healing. And in his own summary of his calling he quoted the words of the prophet saying that he was anointed to announce good news to the poor, release for the prisoners, sight for the blind, and freedom for the oppressed. In these ways Jesus himself taught that the power of God was at work in these deeds of service to men, that in these deeds the will of the Father was being carried out. And when at the very end he wanted to leave an unforgettable picture in the minds of his disciples of what the majesty of God is like, he did it by stooping down to wash their dirty feet. The church will prove its faithfulness to the Lord when it is seen in the same posture.

Second, the church will be faithful to her Lord

when, like him, she bears the marks of suffering. Jesus' own ministry began in service to the needs of men, but it was consummated in suffering. It takes more than those deeds of service to master the powers of evil. They are not mastered by direct attack. They are mastered when the evil that they do is—so to say—absorbed and neutralized by the suffering of God's servants. As Jesus accepted in his own soul and body all that the powers of evil could do to him and offered all his suffering as a willing sacrifice to the Father, so those who follow him are—so far as they are called to do so—ready to accept suffering and shame with him and for him. This acceptance of suffering, and the power to transform suffering into willing sacrifice joyfully offered to the Father, is one of the true and enduring marks of the church.

Third, the church will explicitly bear witness to a reality beyond herself. In this also the church will follow her master. For Jesus not only served and suffered. He also bore witness to the reality of which his deeds were signs. He called men to recognize that these deeds of his were the signs of the Kingdom of God and that these men, therefore, were called for an active response of repentance and faith and hope. In other words, they were not merely to receive or observe these deeds as interesting phenomena but to turn around to face the way God is calling and to commit themselves to go his way. The words of Jesus are as essential to his ministry as his works and so it is with ours.

There is among some Christians a tendency to reject explicit evangelism with the plea that there have been

too many words and that the words have not corre-
sponded with the deeds. There is a plea that what we
need now is not words but deeds. It is true that words
without the deeds that correspond to them are vain, as
James says. But deeds alone are dumb. Our good deeds
do not by themselves bear witness to God's Kingdom.
They only do so if they are in a context of explicit
witness. We have to point beyond our deeds and say
"Don't look at us, don't look at our works, look at
Jesus and follow him. These good works of ours could
never be a substitute for that."

The difficulty, as we know, is that our words are
suspect because we have been guilty more of prosely-
tism than of evangelism. I mean that we have been
more concerned about getting people into our churches
than about getting them enlisted as active agents of
God's Kingdom. It is very easy for us to identify these
two things—to think that getting members for our
church is the same as getting soldiers for Christ's Kingdom. It ought to be, but it is not necessarily so. We
cannot treat church growth as the center of our efforts,
and the reason for this is the same as the reason why
we cannot treat social action as a substitute for evangelism. The reason is that neither our good deeds nor our
life as churches can be put in the place of an explicit
commitment to Jesus Christ. We have to point always
beyond our social programs and beyond our churches
to Jesus Christ himself. What matters is that men
should be committed to him in the battle against the
powers of evil, in his longing that God's will may be
done on earth.

The fourth mark of the church is that it will be a

fellowship in which the life of the Holy City is already enjoyed now in foretaste, a life of freedom, of mutual openness and trust, of mutual care and concern, of sharing all good things in love. I say that the life of the church is to be a community.

In this we see that the church is not merely a means to an end, nor an end in itself, but something different from either of those, a real foretaste of the end. It is not just a means to an end—the church is not just an organization for carrying out programs of service or teaching. Nor, on the other hand, is it an end in itself, an organization existing for the benefit of its members. The second mistake has been a common one. Millions of Christians seem to regard the church as a private society or club which exists to cater to the needs of its members. That is a monstrous caricature of the church as we see it in the New Testament. The first mistake is apt to be made by those who are shocked by the introversion of the church and seek to recall it to its God-given task in the world.

But the truth is that the church is called to be neither a means to an end nor an end in itself; in the language of the New Testament, it is called to be a foretaste, an *arrabon*, an advance payment, of all that God has promised. In the church we are intended to enjoy even now, in a measure, that which is the true end of man, namely fellowship with God and with all men, walking together in the light and delighting in the immeasurable riches of the City of God. And yet all of this is only a foretaste, something which makes us long and pray and work that it may become full and perfect, and that everything unclean, all lying and envying and hatred may be banished so that all men may be able to walk with us in this blessed light.

This means that the church is a fellowship, but an open fellowship. The city has walls, but it has gates open on every side, open day and night as the Book of Revelation reminds us. What gives the city coherence is not a guard at the doors, but a light at the center. All nations are invited to walk in that light, and their kings are invited to bring their treasures into it. Only what is unclean is excluded.

There are some who would make the church a closed fellowship, existing only for its members, suspicious of those outside, anxious to keep them as far away as possible, careful to guard the doors against infiltration.

There are others who would knock down the walls and make no distinction between the church and the world. But that means that the church abandons its vocation to point men to the one goal which makes life meaningful.

The church, I repeat, is to be an open fellowship. If its center is the Lamb, the Lamb is the lamp thereof, as John says. There is no other center. Jesus Christ crucified and risen is the only light of the world.

But all who are willing to turn in the direction of that light are welcome as potential citizens. The doors are open to them day and night. They may be the unbaptized who have seen the light and are trying to follow it, even though they do not yet know that the name of the light is Jesus. They may be the baptized children of Christian homes who have not yet come to the point of taking up the cross themselves to follow the Lamb. Perhaps that means that we should recognize that it does not matter too much at what point baptism is administered if only the direction is steadily towards the center, towards the light. The doors are open and nothing is excluded except what is unclean, what is unfit for fellowship with Jesus.

For the church today, the greatest task is to learn how to be a fellowship which is both open to all men, unafraid of the most intimate contact and cooperation with men of every faith in doing the will of God, and at the same time unshakably centered in Jesus Christ, the Lamb who is the lamp of the city.

That brings me to the fifth point, which is that the church will be a worshiping community. It may be thought that this should have stood first in the list. But I think we understand its meaning better if we take it after we have considered the church as a serving, suffering, witnessing, open community.

The heart of all that I have been trying to say is that the meaning of our life, as human persons and as part of the whole story of nature and history, is to be found in the intention of God, who wills that all things and all men shall come to perfect unity in Jesus Christ, who has promised that this shall be so, and who guides both our personal lives and the life of the world to that end. All that sense of reality which we have about what ought to be but is not yet, derives, I argued, from the fact that this is indeed what God intends and has promised. The reality of all that is good and beautiful and true, but which is caricatured and contradicted by our own experience of the world, is in God. If there is a committed people as the sign and agent and foretaste of what God intends, it can only be so insofar as their life is continually renewed through contact with God himself.

God has revealed his whole mind and purpose in Jesus Christ, supremely in his death and resurrection. In him God's whole heart and will is committed to the healing of the world. And Jesus has invited us to become part of that healing through being part of that dying and rising. He has offered us a share in his baptism and his cup of suffering. Week by week as we celebrate his resurrection, we come together as one fellowship to break the bread and drink the cup which make us partners pledged to him in his dying and his rising. We are bound to him afresh, and as we hear his word expounded we share again his mind and purpose. Through him and with him we offer up ourselves and our possessions and our prayers on behalf of all men, joining our prayers to his that God's Kingdom may come. And then we go out to share completely and fully in the life of the world, not as a separate community seeking our own ends, different from the ends of the world, but simply as those who know what the true end of man is, and who follow Jesus, serving, suffering, and witnessing, so that God's Kingdom may come and God's will may be done, in all men and for all men.

6

The Path of the Disciple

I have tried to put before you a vision of our life, our personal lives and the life of the world, in terms of the intention of God as disclosed to us in Jesus Christ. I have tried to show how what God has disclosed and accomplished and promised for us in Jesus Christ offers us both the possibility of a new life in the Spirit now, and of hope for the world as a beacon to guide us through history. We have now to ask what are the implications of this for each of our own personal lives.

Paul, in his great letter to the Romans, after he has set before his readers the vision of what God has done in Jesus Christ and what he promises to do both for his ancient people Israel and for the nations of the world, begins to bring it home to their personal lives with the words found in Romans 12:1-2:

> Therefore, my brothers, I implore you by God's mercy to offer your very selves to him: a living sacrifice, dedicated and fit for his acceptance, the worship offered by mind and heart. Adapt your-

selves no longer to the pattern of this present
world, but let your minds be remade and your
whole nature thus transformed. Then you will be
able to discern the will of God, and to know
what is good, acceptable, and perfect.

These words may well serve as a guide to us. Note
first the important little word "therefore." It is the
link between what has gone before and what follows. If
you like to put it so, it is the link between doctrine and
life. If it is not there, if doctrine and life fall apart,
God's purpose remains unfulfilled. We may be very
enthusiastic and indeed very fanatical about correct
theology; but if our lives remain as they were, simply
governed by tradition and custom, by what the Bible
calls the world, then of what use is our correct doctrine?

This little "therefore" is like the coupling between
an engine and the train. It is small and it is not
often noticed. But if it is not there the engine may blast
off with a magnificent volume of steam and a thunder-
ing nose, such as only a perfectly orthodox theologian
can produce, but the passengers remain sitting in their
carriages with no chance of going anywhere.

If we are going to talk about Christian doctrine, we
must be asking ourselves honestly and searchingly at
every stage in the discussion: What do these words
mean in terms of my personal life, my family, my
career, my ambitions, my fears, my hopes? If that
coupling is not there, then the talk is just so much
escaping steam.

"Therefore," says Paul, "I beseech you to present your bodies as a living sacrifice."

Notice that he says "your bodies"; he could have said "your souls" and he would have meant the same thing; but he actually said "your bodies." In other words, he is not talking only about something which is interior and spiritual, he is talking about something which concerns our whole selves—our hands, our feet, our brains, our jobs and our lives.

Why should I present myself as a sacrifice? Myself is all that I have. Do I not have a right to enjoy it? Do I not have a right to those things which make life worth living?

The moment we put the question that way, we have an inkling of the answer. What makes life worth living is not the number of good things that we get hold of for our enjoyment. Joy cannot be trapped and held that way. Joy cannot be accumulated in a safe or put in deposit in a bank. Joy is a visitor who comes when she will, and who sometimes calls when we least expect her and sometimes fails to turn up when we were sure she was coming.

God does indeed give us endless joys, but not for hoarding. The point is that our appetite for joy is infinite, but no earthly joy can ever fully satisfy that appetite. Our desires always reach out beyond what we have. However much we have, however great the joys that we have prepared for ourselves, we always, in the moment of enjoyment, want something more. We do not know, perhaps, what it is, but it is something beyond what we have. And so, if we have not learned God's secret, we go on trying to hoard our joys, to grasp at ever new things which we hope will satisfy us, and we end up in misery. The truth is that the good things God has given us to enjoy are an appetizer, not the meal itself. They are intended to refresh us, but also to whet our appetites for the real thing, for the real and lasting joy, which is God himself.

The joy of God is the joy of boundless generosity, of endless giving. God gives us all things freely, but gives them so that we may also learn to give them up. Our joy is not in getting and hoarding, but in getting and giving. The supreme joy is to share both the richness and the generosity of God.

If we understand that we shall understand that beautiful verse in John Keble's hymn:

> *If on our daily course, our mind*
> *Be set to hallow all it find,*
> *New treasures still of countless price,*
> *God will provide for sacrifice.*

God does indeed provide new treasures of countless price every day, more and more wonderful as life goes on. But they are given not to be hoarded but for sacrifice, not to be clutched and hoarded, but to be given back as freely and gladly as God gave them to us.

This is our true joy and this is what Paul calls our reasonable worship. By this we show that we are in the path of Jesus who, for the joy that was set before him, endured the cross and despised its shame. This is a real foretaste of the joy of the City of God, where the servants of the Lamb rejoice to serve him day and night.

It follows from this that the direction of our lives will be the opposite of what is considered normal. It is considered normal in the world to take what one can get, to look at a job, at a career, in terms of its rewards in cash, comfort, and prestige. But those who are the followers of the Lamb, who have their eyes set on the Holy City, will not go that way. They will be nonconformists. "Be not conformed to this world," says Paul, "but be transformed by the renewing of your mind."

The follower of Jesus will be a nonconformist, but he will be a discriminating nonconformist, Paul says. He will not rebel merely for the sake of rebellion. Just as it used to be said that no cause in England could be considered finally lost until it was supported by the Bishop of So and So, so also there are some people who are in principle opposed to anything which appears to be successful or fashionable. I suppose all of us have a natural bias in favor either of what is new or of what is old, depending on which side of forty we are. But this is not what Paul is talking about. He who has his eyes on the City of God, and who is committed to follow Jesus, will have his own judgments to make. His criteria, his sense of proportion, his priorities will be different from those in force around him. This will apply impartially both to what is old and to what is new. In respect of many old and deeply entrenched customs he will surely be an articulate nonconformist.

But there are surely also many things which are hailed as modern in respect of which a follower of Christ will also be a nonconformist. Not everything which is decorated with the adjectives socialist, democratic, and secular is necessarily pointed towards the true welfare of man. Not everything that is technically possible is humanly desirable. The whole attempt to advance the kind of consumer society that depends for its growth on the ceaseless stimulation of unlimited covetousness among the rich, while the poor majority rot in their poverty—this is surely something against which a Christian should be a nonconformist. And that characteristically modern monster, which has a thousand heads but no face, and which goes by the ugly name of bureaucracy, deserves to have the kind of treatment that is accorded to the beast in the Book of Revelation.

I am not trying here to make an outline of Christian ethics for the twentieth century. I only want to make the point that a follower of Jesus Christ will be a discriminating nonconformist. He will make his own judgments about what is going on, whether it is ancient or modern, and he will not just pick them up from the mass media. He will seek always for that renewing of the mind which will enable him to discern what is God's will, what is good and acceptable and righteous. What is called for here is the delicate art of discernment, of discrimination, without which we cannot know what is God's will in each new situation.

This calls for the "renewing of our mind." This is a secret process, which depends on a strong and persistent life of prayer. Without that interior dimension of our lives, without that hidden life of the soul, we cannot learn the kind of discrimination of which Paul speaks, we cannot find this renewing of the mind which will enable us to know what is God's will.

This means that we need a life of prayer in which the stuff of our daily lives is constantly brought into contact with our faith. Our prayer must not be something separated completely from the rest of our life; the coupling between the engine and the train must be intact. In my own experience I have found it necessary to take very simple and practical steps to keep that coupling intact. I find the need to have both my engagement book and my general notebook, along with the Bible and book of prayers, if my times of prayer are to be fruitful. In that quiet hour when we are alone with our Lord, the actual stuff of our daily lives, today's duties and engagements as well as the long-term plans for the future, must be held steadily in the same frame of attention as Christ, his words and his deeds, his dying and his rising. It is only in this way—not in a moment but in steady and continuing discipleship—that our minds can be renewed, so that we can learn to discern what is the will of God, what is good and acceptable and perfect.

But now I come back again to the first part of this text and ask more precisely what is meant by presenting ourselves as a sacrifice, and how this is related to the pursuit of our goals in life. This is a very vital question on which we need to think clearly. I can indicate the point to which I want to draw your attention by putting a number of questions. What do I have a right to look forward to as the result of my efforts? How is God's purpose for all mankind and all creation served by what I do today and tomorrow, which may turn out to be a failure? If I am to be offered up in sacrifice, what is the point of me any-

way? Does this idea not have the effect of cutting the
nerve of any real effort to make a success of my own
life? These are real questions and sometimes they can
be agonizing questions.

We must find the answer to these questions by
looking at Jesus. His cross, his final offering up of his
life to the Father, is the focus and climax of his whole
ministry. But Jesus did not go directly from his baptism to his cross. The cross is indeed the completion of
his baptism. But in between them there are those
crowded months and years of his ministry in which he
labored, agonized, and prayed that his people might
recognize the presence of the Kingdom of God in their
midst, and might accept their vocation to be its agents
and messengers. To the very end he labored to bring his
people to understand what was happening, right up to
the dramatic act of riding into Jerusalem on an ass, and
to the intensely charged teaching of those final days in
Jerusalem. In other words he labored for the doing of
God's will in this world right up to the final limit of
human endurance. Only at that limit do we hear that
final word which marks the completion of the sacrifice: "Father, into thy hands I commend my spirit."
At no point short of that final point did Jesus surren-
der in his battle for the doing of God's will in the
world.

To follow Jesus, therefore, means both of these
things: it means that we spend ourselves and all that we
have for the doing of God's will in this world, in this
secular world, in our job, whatever it may be, right up
to the limit of our powers and of our life. It also means
that at that limit, when we have done all—and only

then—we commit what we have done, with ourselves, into God's hand.

If I may use again the metaphor that I used earlier: from the place where we stand there is a view of the Holy City; but the road to the Holy City goes down into a deep valley of which we cannot see the bottom. There is no bridge. The road goes down into the valley of death. But we follow Jesus in going forward, step by step, over the rough ground on which we are, looking towards the Holy City, even if we are unable to see from where we are how this stony track, on which we are, connects with those golden streets. We go on because we are following Jesus. And even when the track finally disappears from sight, we go down, because we know that he has gone before.

Or, alternatively, if I may put the same thing in the abstract language of propositions, our daily work has two dimensions, both of which have to be taken seriously. On the one hand, our daily work is related to this concrete local and historical situation in which we happen to be—*these* Pharisees and Sadducees and *this* political tension between the Roman power and the revolutionary fervor of the Zealots and the time-serving politics of Herod; *this* concrete situation is *my* home, *my* college, *my* country. This has to be taken with absolute seriousness. It is in this particular situation with all its accidental features that God's will is to be done now as part of God's intention to bring his whole creation into unity in Christ. That is one dimension of our daily work.

But there is also another dimension. My contribution to history may be infinitesimally small. My name may be totally forgotten twenty years from now. But what I do is offered here and now to God as my sacrifice to him. When I have taken careful account of all the concrete factors in the situation; when I have done the utmost that I know how to do to embody the will of God in this particular human situation, I must simply say: "Father, into thy hands I commend this that I have done," and leave the matter with simple confidence in his hands. So we go on, learning day by day a more simple and total obedience, until the day comes for our sacrifice to be complete, and we are ready to commit life itself, along with all that we have done, into God's hands, and still following Jesus, say "Father, into thy hands I commend my spirit."

Perhaps I may be allowed to go back again for a moment to my picture language in order to make my next point. As we set out on our journey the track goes upwards. If you have ever climbed in any high mountains, you will know how in the early stages of the climb, the snowcapped summits are out of sight. You are chiefly conscious of the steep track going up in front of you, and you are exhilarated by the feeling that what is ahead of you is well within your powers. Every now and then you look back to where you started from and feel that you have come a long way.

But then there comes a point where the road begins to go down again. Your powers are not what they were. You are more conscious of the dark valley ahead. There is not the same sense of exhilaration as you see new tasks ahead which are perhaps not so clearly within your powers. But this is also part of the journey, and it has this compensation: the view of the Holy

City is clearer from this part of the road. And that is a source of quiet assurance and joy.

But there is another problem for the traveller. As the day gets hotter, the mists begin to form. Sometimes they blot out the view of the Holy City. Sometimes they are so thick that even the track ahead is invisible. This blackout can sometimes last for days. We do not see the Holy City. We are alone, and when we pray there is no sign that anyone hears.

When that happens there are two things to be said. The first is that we should carry on along the track, one step at a time. We should not try to change direction or look for another track. The time for doing that is when everything is clear. When the mist is down, the only wise thing is to go on faithfully along the track which has served us hitherto.

The second thing is, when we do so, we find that there are footprints on the track. Other people have been this way before. In those hours when the mist has covered everything and we feel that we are alone in the world, the Psalms and the great writings of former pilgrims on this road will assure us that our desolation was theirs also, that they knew what it was to go forward one step at a time with no vision of the goal and no assurance of the presence of Jesus as guide and companion.

If anyone tells you that the life of prayer is one uninterrupted experience of being happy with Jesus, do not follow him. He is not a safe guide. Those who follow the Lamb know that there are stretches of darkness and loneliness and perplexity along the way, and they know also that Jesus himself went that way.

At the end of the journey is the joy of the City of God. He that endures to the end shall be saved, said our Lord. We are saved now, Paul says, but in hope. When our faces are turned towards the City and our feet are set on the track that Jesus trod before us, we are saved by hope. The end is not a private joy but a social joy. It is the joy of God and his people together.

That is why we have to wait, to endure and to serve. It is not our private joy that is the center of the matter; it is that Jesus should see of the travail of his soul and be satisfied. How wrong it is if we think of the end only in terms of heaven or hell for me! Some may wonder why I have not talked more about hell. It is not that I would be so foolish as to deny the possibility of final loss. There is no ground for saying that it is impossible finally to miss the road, to turn away from the light and be left outside the City. But surely the heart of the matter is not my safety and my joy. It is Jesus' joy. It is that he should have the joy of knowing that all for whom he died have come home.

If we have understood that, we will understand why there is need for patience, for endurance and also for action and unceasing commitment to do his will in this world, to work with him to bring the world and all men to the end for which they were created. There will be times when the way is dark and we seem to be alone. But God is faithful who has promised to give us his Kingdom.

God is faithful. That is our security. We know that he can never fail.